AF785975

FSC
www.fsc.org
MIX
Papier aus verantwortungsvollen Quellen
Paper from responsible sources
FSC® C105338

Matthias Schimmel

Communication in the U.K. Budget Airline Industry

How PR affects corporate success

Anchor Academic
Publishing

Schimmel, Matthias: Communication in the U.K. Budget Airline Industry. How PR affects corporate success, Hamburg, Anchor Academic Publishing 2013

Buch-ISBN: 978-3-95489-163-4
PDF-eBook-ISBN: 978-3-95489-663-9
Druck/Herstellung: Anchor Academic Publishing, Hamburg, 2013

Bibliografische Information der Deutschen Nationalbibliothek:
Die Deutsche Nationalbibliothek verzeichnet diese Publikation in der Deutschen Nationalbibliografie; detaillierte bibliografische Daten sind im Internet über http://dnb.d-nb.de abrufbar.

All rights reserved. This publication may not be reproduced, stored in a retrieval system or transmitted, in any form or by any means, electronic, mechanical, photocopying, recording or otherwise, without the prior permission of the publishers.

Das Werk einschließlich aller seiner Teile ist urheberrechtlich geschützt. Jede Verwertung außerhalb der Grenzen des Urheberrechtsgesetzes ist ohne Zustimmung des Verlages unzulässig und strafbar. Dies gilt insbesondere für Vervielfältigungen, Übersetzungen, Mikroverfilmungen und die Einspeicherung und Bearbeitung in elektronischen Systemen.

Die Wiedergabe von Gebrauchsnamen, Handelsnamen, Warenbezeichnungen usw. in diesem Werk berechtigt auch ohne besondere Kennzeichnung nicht zu der Annahme, dass solche Namen im Sinne der Warenzeichen- und Markenschutz-Gesetzgebung als frei zu betrachten wären und daher von jedermann benutzt werden dürften.

Die Informationen in diesem Werk wurden mit Sorgfalt erarbeitet. Dennoch können Fehler nicht vollständig ausgeschlossen werden und der Diplomica Verlag, die Autoren oder Übersetzer übernehmen keine juristische Verantwortung oder irgendeine Haftung für evtl. verbliebene fehlerhafte Angaben und deren Folgen.

Alle Rechte vorbehalten

© Anchor Academic Publishing, Imprint der Diplomica Verlag GmbH
Hermannstal 119k, 22119 Hamburg
http://www.diplomica-verlag.de, Hamburg 2013
Printed in Germany

Acknowledgements

Writing this study would not have been possible without the help and support of numerous people. Firstly, I would like to thank my mentor, Professor Graeme Drummond for his friendly advice and patience. Furthermore, Gail Handyside ensured the success of the primary research for this paper by distributing the invitation E-Mail to the student body of Edinburgh Napier University, which I am very grateful for.

In addition, I would like to thank my parents and family for their guidance and making these studies possible. Last but not least I would like to thank my friends and fellow students for the interesting discussions and their company while writing this paper. Studying at both Edinburgh Napier University and IPAG, Nice, was a memorable experience which contributed to my personal and professional goals. I am thankful that I had the chance to work in this highly international environment, which changed me to being even more open-minded and prepared me for life as a working professional.

Table of Content

Table of Figures

Table of Abbreviations

British Airways	BA
Consumer Behaviour	CB
Dependent Variable	DV
EasyJet	EJ
Edinburgh Napier University	ENU
Frequent Flier Program	FFP
International Air Transport Association	IATA
Low Cost Carrier	LCC
Online Travel Agency	OTA
Public Relations	PR
Return On Investment	ROI
Ryanair	RA

Abstract

The main purpose of this study is to investigate how Public Relations are currently used as a communication tool within the UK budget airline industry, and how the student segment in the UK corresponds to these measures. To gain a holistic understanding of the topic, facts on the UK air transport market are introduced briefly, with a special regard to the two leading budget airlines, Ryanair and EasyJet. Furthermore, the importance of PR for the airline industry is addressed by the defined research aims.

To provide the theoretical background for the conducted research, chapter two focuses on scientific theory, highlighting the areas of Public Relations, Consumer Behaviour and Budget Airlines in particular. By choosing the deductive research approach, nine hypotheses could be developed to contribute to the overall aims and build a basis for the primary research. The latter is an online survey, using the convenient sampling method among the student body of Edinburgh Napier University. Results of the primary research are analysed using SPSS statistical software, conducting frequency distributions, descriptive statistics and chi-square tests.

With regards to the main findings it may be said that price is the most crucial decision factor and thus the strongest communication tool. In addition, there is a shift of recognized communication efforts, away from classic channels as TV or direct mail and towards the corporate homepage and E-Mails, which may be used in a low frequency as to not be perceived as disturbing. All in all, price seems to be more important than service, at least within the student segment. Beside that, the reputation of an airline seems to be important to the respondents, which underlines the need for proper communication efforts. In respect of the limitations and options for further research, there is room to repeat the study with a larger group of participants who are all born and raised in the UK to gain more detailed results. The use of E-Mail in terms of content and frequency might be the most interesting field for future research, as the Internet will be the communication tool of the future.

1. Introduction

This chapter will outline the overall background of the topic. A brief introduction to the UK air transportation business will be given subsequently, to generate a basic understanding of the market at which this paper is aiming. Following this, two leading airlines, namely EasyJet and Ryanair, will be presented as examples of key players in the UK budget carrier market. Then, a brief description of the topic will be given, illustrating the link of PR and the aviation business. Lastly, the aims of this paper are introduced with a concise outlook on the research process.

1.1 The UK Air Transport Market

Mason and Alamdari (2007) divide the travel market into two main segments: the leisure and the business markets. Interestingly, the latter changed significantly as the sale of business tickets started to decline from the year 2000, when many business travellers downgraded to budget airlines. Trends in the leisure market point to splitting up the annual holidays to a number of short trips, increasing the demand for valuable flights. But airline statistics show (BATA, 2010), that after a peak in 2005, the general passenger numbers in the UK are declining to currently level out at 23.3 million in 2010. Davison and Ryley (2010) state that in 2006, 69.5 million visits abroad from the UK had been made, of which 65% were holiday related, plus 17% to visit friends and family. Of the overall number of visits, 81% utilised air travel, which underlines the importance of this way of travel. 79% of all journeys targeted European destinations, using short-haul flights, which is the domain of budget airlines. To sum up the above, the air travel market in the UK is strongly related to leisure travels, which is a growing segment, as holiday and therefore travelling behaviour is changing, creating demand for short-haul flights. Consequently, the following chapters will focus on the two main budget airlines in the UK (Euromonitor, 2009), namely Ryanair (RA), which is Europe's number one low cost carrier (LCC), and EasyJet (EJ), its strongest local competitor.

1.1.1 Ryanair

Euromonitor International (2011) provides very actual and comprehensive information about the Ryanair Holdings Plc. While based in Dublin, Ireland, the company offers its air transportation services in Western and Eastern Europe, with a world air value share of 0,8% in 2010. To keep ticket prices low, RA predominantly operates from secondary airports in Europe. Furthermore, the company secures ancillary revenues with e.g. in-flight sales or car rental agreements. With the acquisition of 29,8% of AerLingus in 2006, RA set its direction to grow strategically, whereas hostile bids in 2006 and 2008 have been cancelled by the European

Commission to prevent the company from establishing dominance in the Irish air transportation market. RA operates on and emphasizes online ticketing, as online sales are much cheaper in terms of staffing; furthermore, commission payments to travel agencies are being avoided.

The Euromonitor International report also conducts a SWOT Analysis (Fine, 2009). RA's leadership position in the market together with their first mover advantages, is identified as key strengths of the organization. In contrast to this, the highly competitive Western European Market and the often-poor customer service as well as employee relationships define RA's weaknesses. Opportunities may be seen in possible strategic alliances with players like Wizzair or SouthWest and in the shift to operate with bigger and more central airports to attract business travellers. Threats to RA's business are increasing aviation taxes and airport fees, as well as volatile fuel prices. Additionally, the report also highlights RA's web strategy, which is of particular interest for this study, as the future of flight bookings will be online (Ruiz-Mafé et al., 2009). Social media will as well be a crucial element of this new travel landscape, offering peer and travel company interaction for decision-making (Euromonitor International, 2011). RA is lagging behind in terms of social media, which is partly due to the fact that its company website receives 180 million visits a year and 99% of all bookings are made online. Likewise, RA need to catch up on the social media trend and avoid PR mistakes like calling a blogger an "idiot and a liar" (Euromonitor International, 2011).

In contrast to the lack of sensitivity towards social media, RA's attention-seeking behaviour seems to be successful. Advertisements run by RA often show content -especially in their print advertising- (Euromonitor International, 2011) causing public backlash and formal complaint. Furthermore, the ads are associated with a low-budget production background while being very attention seeking, particularly when compared to industry competitors. It turns out that the main advantage of RA's advertising is their fast response to current events, such as the royal wedding or the attack of publicity rival EasyJet. RA's marketing in general (Ruddock, 2007) is often an expression of the humour of the companies' charismatic CEO, Michael O'Leary (Creaton, 2004). He is famous for his often direct or even insulting -but entertaining- statements, which are also building the airlines' brand.

Current news (Financial Times, 2011a) and (Financial Times, 2011b) state a rather unfavourable picture of the companies' financial situation. Rising fuel prices and snow-caused airport closures led to loss of more than 10 million Euro. RA still wants to grow further. Beside the efforts made in reaching out for AerLingus, RA indeed did not target specific airlines, but has the ability and will to extend their business and building up new markets. A current example (Reals, 2011) for this is the price war on the Barcelona airports between RA and SpanAir.

1.1.2 EasyJet

Euromonitor International (2009) offers key company data on the EJ LCC, established in 1995. Similar to RA, 95% of all bookings are made via the Internet, which once more demonstrates the strong online-dependence of the business that also will be part of the research of this study. EJ operates 19 bases across Europe, of which 11 are in the UK. To create additional revenue, EJ sells car rentals, hotel and hostel accommodation and travel insurance through its company website. Despite the fact that EasyGroup holding company provides these services as well, EJ decided to develop strategic alliances outside the group, with e.g. Europcar as its main car rental partner.

Euromonitor International's (2009) SWOT Analysis on EJ points out several strengths: While being the number 4 airline in Europe, EJ is the second biggest LCC after RA, with 51% of the passengers originating from outside of the UK. Continued growth is assured through the development of new destinations in Western and Eastern Europe, as well as in North Africa and Turkey. In contrast to RA, EJ operates from the main city airports, which enhances customer convenience and decreases the total travel cost. Furthermore the orange logo has strong brand recognition. Beside the common airline threats, such as the possibility of rising fuel cost and seasonal nature of the business, the report identifies high fix cost as one of the main weaknesses. This is mainly due to the fact that EJ serves primary airports, in contrast to its strongest competitor, RA.

Of all LCC, EJ has been the most successful in attracting business travellers, and targeting this segment is also one of the main opportunities for the future. In addition to this, the company might benefit from expanding their on-board shopping range, as this is a very healthy source of income for the airline. Due to the difficult economic situation, EJ may benefit from the fact that customer needs require less long-haul flights. As all of EJs flights are short-haul, this will satisfy the demand. Threats to EJ may be seen in the increase of taxes and regulations. Furthermore EJ has to adjust its security concept to cope with the current threats, which is a general challenge for the aviation business. Last, EJ recently developed a loyalty scheme, but (Euromonitor International, 2009) it is mentioned that the cheapest price is the only loyalty shown by most consumers. As price may be the marketing tool with the highest impact on the customer, the evaluation of this issue will be part of the research of this study. EJ achieved growth through a combination of takeovers and organic expansion. In

2002 the company acquired the BA subsidiary Go! including a fleet of 25 aircraft. In 2007 the carrier grew by the purchase of GB airways, a British Airways (BA) franchise partner.

Concerning communications and advertising (Euromonitor International, 2009), EJ is following a strong but simple concept. The orange logo is reason for good brand recognition. The image follows a low-cost airline and no-frills service, which is often redefined by poster campaigns, which reflect the simplicity of the whole company concept. Like RA, EJ uses its website as the main communication tool, promoting special prices and targeting registered customers via e-mail newsletters. To enhance brand awareness, EJ appeared in a reality-TV show (Jones, 2007), which followed the day-by-day business of the company.

1.2 PR in the Airline Industry

The field of PR gains increasing importance (Pelsmacker et al., 2010) in today's working environment. With the background of an economic crisis, companies need to be aware of their communications mix and push their marketing measures to stay in and enhance their business. Furthermore, good media relations can positively influence a company's public image and should be desirable, as this is a marketing channel, which does not cause additional budget constraints. With a regard to budget airlines, it is thus of interest to investigate what the customers' perception of the company's PR efforts is. PR is an important tool within the promotional mix. It is a framework, which is applied to achieve tactical competitive advantage. Especially the two previously introduced key players in the UK LCC market, RA and EJ, distinguish themselves with unusual and conspicuous PR measures, such as using e.g. unusually informal language in their press conferences, or trying to insult one another in their advertising campaigns. It is the desire of being different -not necessarily being better- that seems to drive the companies' PR efforts. Communication in the highly competitive LCC market means a daily fight for customers, most often using its utmost powerful tool: the low ticket price.

There is support to explore this topic further due to the lack of empirical research concerning the predefined areas. The paper is focusing on this gap within the corresponding literature of PR as a communication tool in the UK budget airline industry. Subsequently, the research aims will be introduced to build a basis and guidance for the study that will be carried out for this paper.

1.3 Research Aims

The overall aim of the study is to generate an understanding of how Public Relations are currently used as a communication tool within the UK budget airline industry, and how the student segment in the UK corresponds to these measures. Furthermore, the following five objectives will be assessed in detail:

a) The influence of PR on the consumer decision-making process shall be evaluated, including a focus on distribution channels, such as company websites or ticket price comparison websites.

b) The use of PR as a communication tool with specific interest in the budget airline industry shall be displayed.

c) The importance and perception of PR as a communication tool shall be measured, with a focus on the student segment.

d) Marketing of Services: Do consumers favour online bookings? Implications on further marketing strategies and the future of print advertising media shall be developed.

e) The selection factors and stimuli of a student customer choosing an airline shall be evaluated to form a holistic picture of the decision making process.

Based on the overall aim and the five additional objectives introduced above, hypotheses will be developed and presented in chapter 3.1. The hypotheses will then be researched using an online questionnaire. The analysis of the obtained data will be given in chapter 4, where findings will be displayed and a connection to the subsequent chapter, the literature review, will be made. Lastly, the conclusion -chapter 5- will link all, aims, hypotheses and findings, to draw implications for working professionals. The following section will provide the reader with the literary background of scientific theory linked to the topic.

2. Literature Review

This chapter will provide the reader with the background and academic theory related to the topic. The fields of Public Relations, Consumer Behaviour and Budget Airlines in general have been identified as most relevant and will be assessed in light of the study topic and aims.

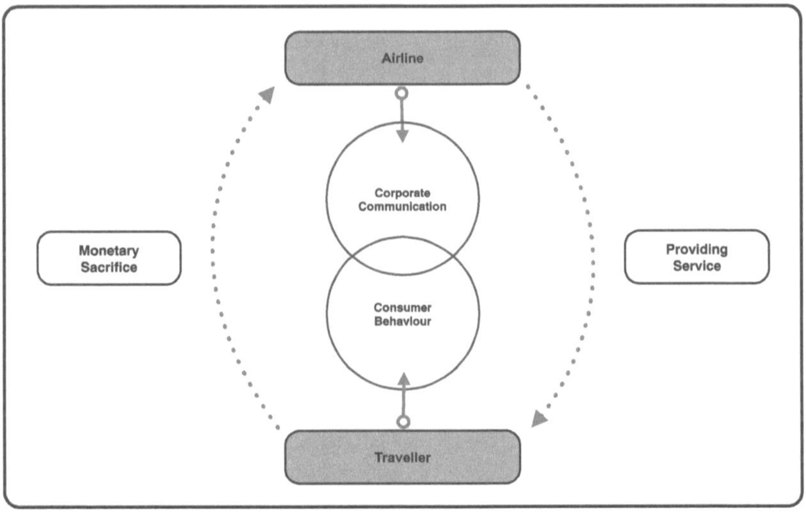

Fig. 2.1: Airline / Consumer Relational Concept

The adjacent **Fig. 2.1** may display the basic interrelations of the different elements, which will be the content of the subsequent chapters. The following chapter will give an insight into the field of Public Relations, with a focus on the airline industry.

2.1 Public Relations

Public Relations (PR) is used in a wide range of industries, each of them requiring different skills and competencies. As a result to that fact, there is no general applicable definition of PR, but Tench and Yeomans (2009, p. 4) cite an academic definition of Harlow, which outlines the topic quite well: "Public Relations is a distinctive management function which helps establish and maintain mutual lines of communication, understanding, acceptance and cooperation between an organisation and its publics; involves the management of problems or issues; helps management to keep informed on and responsive to public opinions; defines and emphasises the responsibility of management to serve the public interest; helps management keep abreast of and effectively utilise change; serving as an early warning system to help anticipate trends; and uses research and ethical communication techniques as its principal tools."

Tench and Yeomans (2009) mention the main three tasks of PR or corporate communication, according to Fombrun and Van Riel. First, management communication is aimed at the development of a shared vision, the establishment and maintenance of trust in the leadership, management of change and the motivation of employees. Second, marketing communication supports the sale of goods and services, including advertising, sales promotion, direct mail, personal selling, online and mobile marketing as well as market-oriented PR or publicity. Last, organisational communication usually covers activities at a corporate level, which do not have to be located in the PR department, e.g. public affairs, investor relations or corporate advertising.

Haywood (1991) gives a very holistic insight on the various fields of PR. It is interesting, that those campaigns are most successful, are "closest to reality", generating credibility for the company. In his opinion, an effective promotional campaign must coordinate all the elements that contribute to the corporation personality. Haywood concludes that PR is supporting marketing in many areas, namely awareness improvement, projecting credibility, combating competition, evaluating new markets, creating direct sales leads, reinforcing the effectiveness of sales promotion and advertising, motivating the sales force and distributors as well as wholesalers and retailers, the introduction of new products or services, building brand loyalty, dealing with customer concerns and in many other ways.

Haywood also refers to the close link of PR measures to sales support. Due to PR activity, the sales staff will spend less time and effort with the customer, as the reputation of the company is already well established. If the customer knows the company name due to its appearance in a specific professional journal, this journalistic pre-selection will support the whole communication process. In the same way, PR might help the company or brand getting a good name in a potential market to open up new sales opportunities.

Xavier et al. (2005) demonstrate that PR professionals show various ways to contribute towards organizational goals; they point out the ambiguity if these reporting structures are matching real outcomes. To tackle this problem, the study combines evaluation practices and industry data to make PR accountable. The findings are that practitioners are still focusing on outputs, not outcomes of PR, and continue to rely heavily on media-based evaluation methods.

The work of L'Etang et al. (2007) focuses on the interrelation between tourism and PR. They show that the field of tourism is rather unexplored by PR research, which also shows that this study will be a scientific contribution that will help to fill this research gap. L'Etang et al.

(2007) suggest that future research may develop an agenda that incorporates cultural and critical perspectives, drawing on media sociology, cultural studies and tourism literature. In their opinion, tourism PR shall not only focus on traditional instrumental perspectives, but also recognize the "bigger picture", involving a broader social, political and cultural perspective. By applying that, tourism public relations research would overcome the restricted traffic between other disciplines.

Macleod (2010) evaluated the connection of PR with the Internet. She emphasises the point that the process of information gathering and reputation building has been simplified, as there is a shift from the earlier process -involving the analysis of media outlets and stakeholder opinions- to give the power of reputation building to the hands of small groups or even individuals, which may communicate without boundaries in time and space. This fact is particularly interesting for this study, as the majority of today's airway travel tickets are sold online (Ruiz-Mafé et al., 2009). Due to the strong evolution of Internet usage, Macleod mentions that the more known a brand name is, the more vulnerable it is. This could mean an Achilles heel to some companies, as consumers tend to exchange information faster.

Public Relations may affect companies in various ways. Alves and Barbot (2010) found interesting interrelations between the announcements of new routes of travel from EasyJet that may affect the share price of Ryanair. The impacts may be positive or negative. At the core of this paper is the finding that route announcements -which are PR measures- may be used to influence stock prices of competitors.

Public Relations come to importance in particular when companies have to handle a crisis or critical situation. Greer and Moreland (2003) put their attention to the online crisis communication of United and American Airlines, following the September 11. terrorist attacks. Based on crisis communication theory they examine how the two airlines use their websites as a communication tool within three weeks after the incidents. On the one hand, the carriers communicated clear facts. On the other, they communicated their commitment to the event with a series of condolence messages.

The work of Ni (2006) also focuses on the impact of PR, while relating it towards companies' organizational strategies. His qualitative research is based on interviews with 33 Chinese PR managers, to explore relationships as organizational resources and their contribution to strategy implementation. Ni found that relationships bear the following key features as resources and advantages: Valuable, rare, difficult to imitate and hard to substitute.

Processes within companies benefit from structured planning, as it identifies long-term opportunities as well as threats and mobilizes the resources to address them. As a result,

Forbes (1992) emphasizes the link of strategic management to PR. He mentions that in a strategically operated company, the senior PR manager has the task to harmonize all external and internal publics. This goal may be achieved by applying a six-step process. The first step is to scan and build awareness of the future. It will be to the organizations benefit to predict trends covered within the PEST-Analysis (Basu, 2009) for one decade ahead. Since it is impossible to certainly predict the future, the next step includes scenario planning for optimistic and pessimistic developments, as well as a situation in between the two, to function as a basis for contingency planning.

As a result, a mission statement might be written on the review of the possible scenarios. It should be re-assessed annually to cope with current changes. Fourth, this statement may be translated into objectives and policies that serve as a framework to the overall strategy. Step 5 covers the implementation of the strategy, by the execution of detailed action plans and the allocation of budgets to carry out the objectives set by senior management. Last, the strategy needs to be reviewed and updated where necessary. The application of this process helps organisations to stay ahead and enables them to respond to upcoming business developments in a flexible manner.

The work of Hauss (1993) is of particular interest for this study, as she gives implications on how the impact of PR may be measured. It is said that the media has a lot of influence on the way people think, buy and vote. To show how the impact of media content can be measured, research had been conducted during the 1992 presidential election in the USA. Scientists evaluated the influence of good and bad news and how people would respond to this with their votes, finding significant correlations. Another way to measure the PR impact was the link between inquiries and the ROI of product-sales driven organizations. The Windows-based program "Sales Projector" lets users estimate the amount of actual closed business a company's sales leads are likely to produce. The software is able to distinguish the number of leads coming in with a relation to PR or other Marketing efforts, with the result that PR is the number two lead generator after trade shows. With the use of the program it was proven that PR turns into sales at a predictable rate.

Vogel (1994) puts a focus on how mass communications work and introduces the "Relativity Model of Mass Communications". According to him, PR experts decide on budget allocations of corporate messages through the answer of three questions: First, how important are the messages for the company? Second, how important are the messages we want to emphasize to the people we want to reach? Third, how well informed are those people about these messages? By using this approach it is assured that budget is spent on the messages that are important for the company as well as for the audience.

According to the "Relativity Model of Mass Communications", there are two main market segments for each message. One is the audience that is interested in the topic and agrees with the authors' point of view. The other are the people that think the message is important, but do not have any distinct opinion about it. The rest of the audience is simply not the market for the message. However, the model categorizes the audience as follows: active opponents, active supporters, disinterested opponents, disinterested supporters, potential converts and the uninvolved. Only the active supporters and potential converts are good candidates for messages under normal circumstances. After having classified the audience in this manner, communication priorities can be set in a cost effective way, as the budget may be allocated with the groups that expect the most favourable impact. This leads to the setup of a successful strategy, which was predefined earlier in this chapter.

How challenging it may be to measure the actual impact of PR procedures is as well mentioned in the research of Beth (1994). According to him, PR may have two general sides - internal and external- where numbers in sales, productivity and profit are being supported through the work of PR professionals to seize every opportunity. These numbers symbolize the behaviour of people. Just as sales represent the behaviour of consumers, productivity reflects the behaviour of employees. Beth argues further, that a PR specialist focusing on employee relations may have an indirect positive impact on the companies' bottom line by improving employee morale, thereby increasing productivity and lowering the number of absence days. The author mentions that the key drivers to an improvement of employee morale are recognition, money and information. As PR may affect recognition and information, it may as well have a positive effect on the companies' bottom line.

Last, another crucial role of PR is the communication during a crisis. An example is the "Good Words" campaign of American Airlines (Downing, 2004), which was offered internally to employees after the 9/11 terrorist attacks, in order to support emotional needs. But instead of helping to handle the crisis like in the previous example, PR may also help to prevent critical developments. Christen (2005) attributes the failure of AT&T to properly manage their restructuring phase to two main reasons: First, AT&T was not able to construct a shared system of beliefs that made sense of the need to downsize. Second, the company demonstrated an inability to cope with the conflicting demands of key external publics. Proper PR management would have been able to identify and solve these issues beforehand, leading to a streamlined process and a better corporate image.

To conclude the above, it becomes clear that PR is a crucial factor to the success of a business. It helps to build up a shared vision, helps to drive sales and product awareness. Technical development might shift values to give power to a few opinion leaders; that is why PR professionals need to focus on online communication. PR needs shall be part of companies' strategic planning to ensure long run success. Bearing in mind that PR is that essential, it is remarkable that the field of Tourism PR is rather unexplored. Furthermore, the difficulty of measuring PR impacts has been pointed out by Hauss (1993) and Beth (1994), who either measured voters' opinions with a regard to current news or referred to rather soft factors like employee morale improvement, leading to bottom line improvements. The next section will address Consumer Behaviour literature, as well partially regarding the airline industry.

2.2 Consumer Behaviour

Evans et al. (2006) cover the various aspects of Consumer Behaviour (CB) as a whole, by assessing individual and group aspects of the topic and linking them to integrated approaches of CB. As for the individual, the main shopping motives for buying a ticket from an LCC, the pleasure of bargaining, anticipated utility -provided benefits- and choice optimization -the right product to satisfy demand- may be identified. According to the authors, consumers follow a certain hierarchy of communication effects when responding to marketing actions: exposure, attention and perception, learning attitude, action and post-purchase. PR measures are then related to the beginning of this hierarchy, the exposure and the attention part. Evans et al. (2006) further write about social groups, which are of importance for the research of this study, as it will be targeted to the informal group of students living in the UK. Many of them will also be members of virtual groups in online communities, which can be linked to company PR in form of e.g. Facebook groups as well.

Wright (2006) highlights the importance of CB. He mentions that if management understands customer responses better than the competition, this will generate a source of knowledge, leading to competitive advantage. As markets open and technologies develop, they also become more competitive and less product driven. To achieve and maintain a leading position in an environment like this, companies have to understand the variety of internal and external influencing factors as well as problem-solving processes that will affect the product, brand and service purchase decisions. This topic is directly linked to (Singleton, 2010) the concept of customer segmentation, as all marketing measures may be used and targeted more efficiently if the company is aware who their customers are in terms of e.g. gender, age or disposable income.

Mudie and Pirrie (2006) focused their work on a crucial element of CB, the marketing of services, which also relates to the nature of the airline business. Core to the business with services is that they are intangible and cannot be owned or processed, meaning that the potential consumer is often unable to perceive the service before -and sometimes during and after- the service delivery. This implicates that the customer has to be physically present in many cases to benefit from the "production" of a service. Mudie and Pirrie further mention the perishability of services, meaning that e.g. unsold airline seats or empty hotel rooms may not be reclaimed, as services are performances and cannot be stored. Beside the well-known 4-P marketing concept (Jobber, 2010), which includes Product, Price, Promotion and Placement, the marketing of services may be extended to a 7-P concept (Mudie and Pirrie, 2006) to better respond to the characteristics of services, namely People, Physical evidence and Process. Beside that, the authors highlight the role of services communication, stating that communication can add value to the service in the eyes of the consumer. But marketing also has to respect service characteristics. Along with the previously mentioned features, like intangibility and perishability, the heterogeneity of services plays a role, which can be addressed by communications, often with the Internet (Sterne, 2000) as a supportive tool.

Euromonitor International (2010b) presents very good information on consumer lifestyles in the UK. As the research of this study will be carried out among a UK-based student body, this study will provide a valuable background to understanding the participants. The authors identify a clear trend towards Internet affinity among UK consumers, with 70% of the households having an internet-enabled PC. The outlook given is that this number will rise in the future, as the UK government aims to make fast broadband Internet available to all UK households by 2012. This development is also supported by a decrease in IT hardware prices. As a result, e-commerce revenues almost doubled during the research between 2005 and 2009. Furthermore, 50% of the UK consumers book their holidays online, which displays the strong Internet affinity of the business.

Concerning air transport (Euromonitor International, 2010b), 37% of all flights in the UK in 2010 were short haul, whereas 18% were long haul and 8% domestic. This shows that airlines like RA and EJ compete in the largest segment: the short haul flights. These figures did not change significantly compared to 2006 and 2008, which indicates that the demand on the air transportation market in the UK is not very volatile, apart from impacts of the economic downturn, particularly in early 2009.

The research of Mason and Alamdari (2007) links the future trends of LCCs and CB. By using the Delphi method, they assessed the viewpoints of 26 air transportation experts to derive their findings. The consensus opinion of the experts was that network carrier consolidation would reduce the main market to three key players, competing with two to three large LCCs. The authors further imply that business class will disappear on short haul flights, as business travellers will seek better value for money. With a regard to leisure travelling, the trend would move away from one or two major holidays; instead, leisure travellers might prefer multiple short-duration holidays during the year, due to the decrease in fares.

Gallarza and Saura (2006) investigated on university students' travel behaviour, with an emphasis on the influence of perceived value on CB. Because the research of this study will focus on UK university students, their findings are of particular interest. The managerial implications of the authors are that price policies are not always the more prominent factor when evaluating tourism experiences. Furthermore, the authors state that among the diverse cost of consuming, time and effort may overcome the monetary sacrifice and therefore recommend reconsideration for under-pricing policies, particularly in the airline sector. With a regard to the LCC market, this is a very interesting statement, as the importance of value for money and pricing will be part of the research of this study. Core finding of Gallarza and Saura was that high quality does affect customer value perceptions, leading to greater customer satisfaction, which strengthens the intention to repurchase and recommend.

Considering that both of the main UK LCC competitors -RA and EJ- tend to use offensive advertising, the work of Chan et al. (2007) is of interest, as it delivers results to the cross-cultural perception of offensive ads. Although the study is carried out among German and Chinese students, implications for the UK market may be derived. The findings of the authors were rather mixed, but showed that the Chinese participants were more sensitive to offensive advertising and rejected it stronger than the German contributors. In addition, the Chinese were more likely to find an advertisement convincing and informative. The perceptions between the cultures are differentiated, but pictures with sexually oriented body images received the most negative ratings and led to significant impact on consumers' intentions to reject either a product or a brand. Customer personality and emotions are the core of the research of Gountas and Gountas (2007), who found a direct relationship between the consumers' personality orientation, emotional characteristics and self-reported satisfaction of the service experience.

Dolnicar et al. (2011) carried out a study on the key drivers of airline loyalty. The report - analysing the views of 687 passengers- identifies frequent flyer membership, price, the status of being a national carrier and word-of-mouth reputation as the most significant determinants of whether a airline customer is loyal to a company or not. The importance of the previously mentioned determinants varies between the different traveller segments, as e.g. business travellers may show a stronger interest in loyalty programs than casual or leisure travellers. An interesting fact is that satisfaction emerged as a key driver of airline loyalty in none of the models the authors calculated. In contrast to Gallarza and Saura (2006), Dolnicar et al. (2011) mention that leisure travellers especially are highly influenced by the price factor, which underpins the need of clarification of this topic with further research.

Aksoy et al. (2003) discuss airline services marketing of one domestic and four foreign airlines in Turkey from the customers' point of view. The authors conclude that the differences in customer profiles and expectations are valuable clues for carriers in order to understand their customers and target them better in marketing strategies. The respondents were categorized in different groups, determining e.g. their sex, age and education. Each category was then compared on differences in perception between the domestic and foreign airlines. Aksoy et al. found, that there are significant differences between passenger groups using foreign or domestic airlines to the same destinations, with respect to their demographic profiles, behavioural characteristics and understanding of airline service dimensions. According to the research, the domestic airline users tend to be older, better educated, more frequent travellers and rather internationally oriented. The most crucial services mentioned are food & beverage services, personnel, cabin features, in-flight services, country of origin and promotion, punctuality and speed.

Hess and Adler (2011) compare four different datasets of previous studies in order to derive trends in air travel behaviour. One of the emerging topics was the decrease in customers' willingness to pay measures. This is explicable by the market development, which offers more and more low-cost options for the customer, leading to higher price-sensibility. Linked to this are the reduction of frequent flyer benefits and the increased use of online ticketing, as well as the lack of service differentiation among major US airlines.

Jen et al. (2011) highlight airline passengers' behavioural intention. Core to their model is that airline managers who want to obtain favourable behavioural intentions from passengers by providing better service may ensure that the service is actually improving passengers' satisfaction, e.g. raising positive emotion. According to their findings, perceived value is the most important predictor of passenger behavioural intentions, and perceived value is mainly affected by perceived costs.

The work of Tuzovic (2010) relates to the investigation in online dysfunctional customer behaviour, caused by frustration incidents among members of loyalty programs in the airline industry, which generates negative word-of-mouth. This is of particular interest, as customer loyalty programs have become important marketing instruments. They enhance the companies' chances to know more about their customers, identify most valuable customers and to differentiate the treatment of those high-value customers. Tuzovic points out that airlines mostly ignored if members of these loyalty programs had negative experiences that led to their frustration. He further mentions that the accumulation of frequent flier miles is an important reason for customers to participate in Frequent Flier Programs (FFP). According to the psychological value of these miles, the refusal, reduction or postponement of the promised benefits results in customer frustration and causes the pre-mentioned dysfunctional behaviour in online feedback forums. As a result, the whole customer relationship may be weakened.

To summarise, Consumer Behaviour is of certain interest for this study, as PR measures target consumers and try to ensure a certain outcome. CB delivers the background on e.g. reasons of purchase or perceptions, often linked with social groups. Company knowledge in CB may lead to a better understanding of the customer, which may lead to competitive advantage. Since the airline industry is marketing services, knowledge of the customer base is crucial. As 50% of UK customers book their holidays online, the strong Internet relation of the business is evident. Pricing is identified as one of the major issues in airline CB, especially with a regard to consumers' willingness to pay -which is decreasing- and loyalty matters. While having considered the theory of Public Relations as well as Consumer Behaviour in light of the airline business, the subsequent section will discuss the topic of Budget Airlines.

2.3 Budget Airlines

In addition to chapter 1.1, which outlined the UK air transport market in a wider context, this chapter will relate to academic theory and research in the budget airline segment.

Shaw (2007) relates the topics of airline marketing and management in his very holistic and recognized work. As the dimensions of this literature review are limited, the following will focus on Shaw's view on Porter's five forces for the airline market, to generate an overview and introduction on the topic. Core to Porter's model are the industry competitors, which can be seen as Europe's long-established airlines, especially in the short-haul markets. Since April 1997, EU airlines have competed in a single market, with loose controls over entry, capacity and fares, allowing LCCs to grow. Video- and telephone conferences, as well as E-Mails may have a substitution effect, resulting in a decrease of business-related travelling. Furthermore, surface transport, e.g. rail services also raise important substitution issues.

New entrants in particular affect Europe's low-fare scene. They are often forced to use uncongested airports, which are regularly located at a distance to desirable destinations.

Therefore slot constraints may comfort existing airlines. Last, entering the airline industry requires high monetary and staff resources, which limits the amount of potential start-ups. The power of customers is crucial to determining the profitability for firms in any industry. Customer bargaining power can be seen in company deals, where loyalty is traded for tremendous discounts. This changed the industry, as travelling customers turned into powerful negotiators. The power of suppliers is significant in the airline industry, as many contractors have a position, which is at least similar to a monopoly, such as Air Traffic Control or Airport Services. In addition to this, airline fleet planning might be strongly dependent on supplier resources.

Doganis (2006) provides a good overview of the airline business, including implications on LCCs and the strong e-commerce relation of the industry. Doganis states that judging on individual factors such as legroom comfort and catering cleanliness of cabin crew, all LCC were considered among the worst. In contrast to this, they were rated best in terms of value for money. This brings up the assumption that passengers tend to accept comfort disadvantages, as long as a good price/performance ratio is guaranteed. Concerning the budget airline market in the UK, Doganis identifies RA and EJ as key players, which initially competed with BA's GO and KLM's Buzz low-cost subsidiaries, which then had been taken over by the two dominant LCCs as well. In an intra-European comparison, the UK and Ireland show the highest domestic LCC penetration, with over 40% of all seats sold being low-cost. The airline industry in general could not exist without complex IT systems, as they are necessary for online sales, electronic ticketing and loyalty programs. The electronic marketplace offers consumers fast, unlimited and efficient access to information on airline services, timing and prices, and the ability to make real time reservations and payments. Doganis relates this development to economic theory by stating that greater knowledge among consumers means greater market power. A result of this, e-commerce makes the marketplace more transparent and competitive, which may evolve to a serious threat for some airlines.

Dobruszkes (2006) mentions three general reasons for the existence of LCC. First, air transport is a cyclical industry, which is strongly correlated to economic cycles, involving a high fix-cost level due to aircraft-ownership. Second, a large proportion of the population is limited in its use of air transport, as a result of increasing ticket fares. Last, the liberalizations of the air transport sector allow free creations of new services and therewith support the foundation of new airlines. These facts lead to the implication that LCC benefit from economic downswings, which triggers the use of budget airlines due to the lower disposable income of the customers. But the cheaper prices are only achieved with sacrifices: Dobruszkes explains that LCC personnel are paid less then regular airline employees, all while having a higher workload.

Callison and Seltzer (2010) gave a best practice example on successful airline PR. Their research corresponds to the communication conduct of Southwest Airlines, a company widely recognized for their PR efforts. As a result, the authors conclude that the key drivers for successful communication are practitioner responsiveness and accessibility to reporters. The combination of these two factors enhances a positive perception in the eyes of journalists and thus the corporate image, which also positively influences consumers.

Koo et al. (2011) talk about the online distribution of airline tickets and whether it is favourable for airlines to adopt single or multi channels. As today's travel environment is widely affected by the Internet, main airline ticket distribution channels are the company's own website, and online travel agency platforms (OTA) as e.g. Expedia or Travelocity. Even though the distribution via an OTA is linked with higher distribution cost, the airlines benefit from exposure to a broader consumer base, which will generate additional sales and spread risk. In contrast to this, some airlines, e.g. RA and EJ, decided to focus on only one channel and use only the corporate website for distribution. Koo et al. (2011) conclude that airlines are less likely to use OTA support if they have a loyal customer base, or if the OTA platform is highly competitive. It is an interesting fact that airlines that do not use OTA platforms often outperform their competition in terms of profitability. Koo et al. (2011) also state, that if the share of loyal customers inversely relates to price, there is a rather limited possibility that airlines join an OTA platform. Key to a successful pricing strategy is therefore the action in respect to consumers' price sensitivity, in order to broaden the loyal customer base, which will use the corporate brand.com pages instead of an OTA. Furthermore, using a multichannel distribution strategy would enhance the airline's coordination issues.

Chang and Chang (2010) use structural equation models to carry out a survey among airline customers who experienced service failure and recovery. They conclude that both interactional and procedural justice influence recovery satisfaction, but mention that the latter does not have any influence on customer loyalty. The results of their study confirm the existence of the mediating role of recovery satisfaction in the relationship between service recovery and overall satisfaction in the airline industry.

Forgas et al. (2010) compare LCCs and traditional airlines by identifying the antecedents of airline user loyalty. Oliver (1997) defines loyalty as "the highest level of commitment, implying the transition from a favourable predisposition (affective loyalty) to a repeated purchase commitment (conative loyalty) as a prior step to the action of purchase." Bearing this definition in mind, Forgas et al. (2010) conclude that the principal antecedent of conative loyalty is affective loyalty, irrespective of company type, but there are differences in the antecedents of loyalty between LCCs and traditional airlines. Trust seems to play a more important role with LCCs. An explanation to this could be that passengers associate the low price with lower quality, and when this service is chosen, the consumer might need a bonus of trust and security of service. In all cases, emotional value is the element that generates most satisfaction. Significant differences may be found by looking at the antecedents of satisfaction. For LCCs, the quality of service and the monetary price are identified as the key drivers of loyalty. For traditional airlines, the professionalism of personnel is of higher importance. The authors also highlighted the role of brand image in terms of social value. In both airline segments, the brand directly influenced customer loyalty and satisfaction. Especially in the LCC segment, the brand has a strong impact on trust as well. This is interesting in particular, as the brand image is the result of the communication efforts of a company, linked with the actual passengers' travelling experience. The authors recommend that airlines might put great attention to detail when providing the service, as this could help to reinforce satisfaction and trust as well as affective loyalty.

Similar to the previous authors, Chiou and Chen (2010) pick out passengers' intentions towards traditional and LCCs as a central topic. The research, carried out among passengers of China's first budget carrier, Spring Airlines, identifies service perception as a latent variable with the most significant influence on intentions, using full-service or traditional carriers. With a regard to LCCs, this influence is smaller. Conversely, service value emerged as the greatest influencing factor on intentions for possible LCC passengers. This implies that the low-fare strategy remains to be the top priority. The authors conclude that an increase in service without the offer of low prices would not be sufficient to positively stimulate passenger numbers, considering the background of the passengers of Spring Airlines, who take no-frills service for granted and are therefore a lot more price sensitive.

To sum up the above, LCCs do have a great importance in today's travel environment. Although there are substitutes through highly developed communication devices or e.g. rail service, 40% of all airline seats sold in the UK are allocated to budget airlines. Passengers seem to accept comfort disadvantages in order to obtain a valuable price/performance ratio. Due to the strong Internet relation of the business, with LCCs often exclusively selling through their corporate website, the market evolves to be competitive and with high consumer power. The loyalty to an LCC is linked to the key drivers of service quality and the monetary price, bearing in mind that an increase in service without a decrease in price would not trigger passenger numbers to rise.

3. Methodology

This chapter will provide an overview on the primary research of this paper. The research approach will be explained with a regard to the method used and the sample of participants. Furthermore, the methods of data analysis are explained and limitations of this paper will be evaluated. Bryman and Bell (2007) discuss the "process of deduction" in research, which outlines the research concept of the author for this study. Figure 3.1 graphically explains the major steps of linking scientific theory with new findings, generated by primary research. The author extended the model by summarising the six single steps to three major phases.

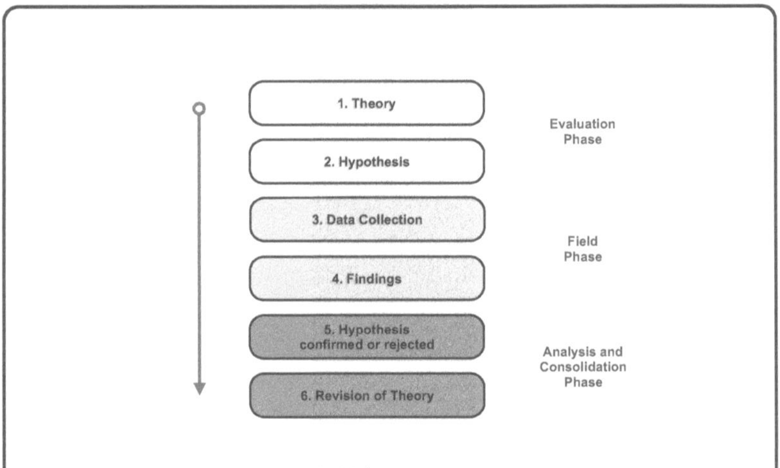

Own graphics, deduction process taken from: Bryman and Bell (2007)

Fig. 3.1: The Process of Deduction

Cooper and Schindler (2006) also point out the importance of reflective thinking during the research process. It consists of sequencing induction and deduction in order to explain a puzzling condition by hypothesis. They state that researchers think of the process of science as an orderly method that combines induction, deduction, observation, and hypothesis testing into a set of reflective thinking activities.

3.1 Research Approach and Hypotheses

As mentioned previously, the author follows the deductive research approach (Saunders et al., 2009). According to the process shown in Fig. 3.1, hypotheses are developed along the existing theory and will then be tested (Shi and Tao, 2008). Fig. 3.1.1 introduces the hypotheses and explains how they are related to the overall aims, which may be found in more detail in 1.3.

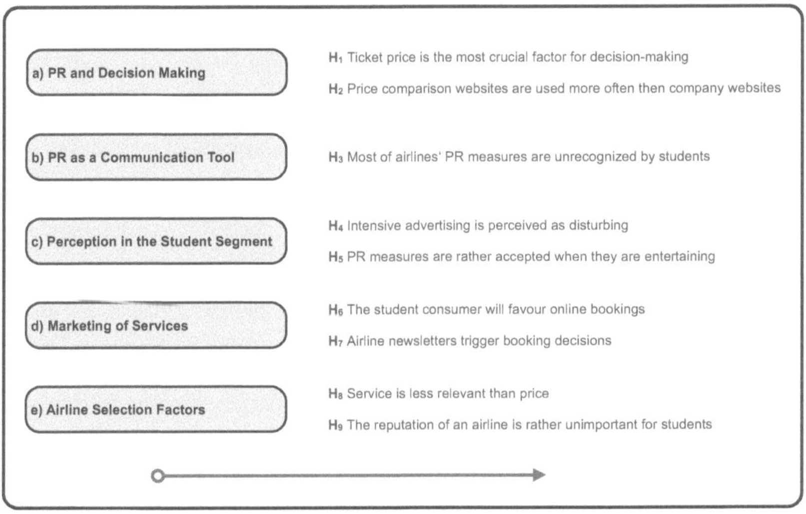

Fig. 3.1.1: Hypotheses

The decision for the deductive approach is reasonable, as it provides a clear outline of the research process for the author. The framework allows to carefully prepare the next research step and helps to avoid the "back and forth between data and theory" that would be required while applying the inductive approach (Bryman and Bell, 2007). The deductive approach may contain disadvantages or dangers as well (Engel and Schutt, 2005). There is the possibility that the data obtained may not fit with the original hypothesis or that new theoretical findings may be published earlier than the conducted research.

3.2 Research Method

Among the wide range of research methods used, only two can be mainly identified in the literature, namely the quantitative and qualitative approaches (Creswell, 2009). The research for this paper is following the quantitative method. Based on positivist and neopositivist thought, quantitative research is known to yield trustworthy results. In addition, it is said (Hoy,

2009) that quantitative methods are more accurate than the qualitative ones, as they are more controlled and omit factors that may negatively influence the research results. They are based on logical reasoning and statistics. One of the major reasons for using the quantitative approach is the use of scientific procedures in order to generate findings. By taking these procedures as a guideline, the author will be able to gather data corresponding to the research aims and hypotheses of this paper, in an accurate and non-biased manner (Vogt, 2007).

Hussey and Hussey (1997) mention that the quantitative approach would be relatively less time consuming and that it is less expensive to collect the required data, which displays core advantages of the method. To sum up the above, the research for this paper will follow the quantitative approach, which allows the author to gather a vast amount of data in order to increase the chances of generalisation and drawing conclusions. However, no research method is flawless and technical problems as well as demand persistence may appear during the research process (Cooper and Schindler, 2006). The process of measurement may be criticised as well, as it can be argued that it has a false meaning of precision and accuracy. Bryman and Bell (2007) also believe, that -depending on the questionnaire and the set of actions- the link between the research and everyday life might be comparably limited.

Quantitative and qualitative methods are not the only approaches that may be discovered in the literature. Another widely recognized method is the case study approach, which may be used to assess a specific phenomenon (Yin, 2009; Swanborn, 2010), to generate findings and draw questions for future research projects (Saunders et al., 2009). However, Bryman and Bell (2007) argue that this approach may show a lack of external validity and generalizability of findings. By evaluating the advantages and disadvantages of the different approaches with regard to the research aims of this paper, the author was led to the decision that the quantitative approach seems to be most applicative to generate valuable outcomes.

3.2.1 Data Collection and Tool Design

As shown previously, several methods or strategies for data collection exist. The wide range of data collection tools consists of surveys, interviews, experimentation, case studies, diary methods and observation (Bryman and Bell, 2007, Cooper and Schindler, 2006; Saunders et al., 2009). This study follows the deductive approach and uses an online survey as the data collection tool, which is one of the most applied ways to capture data when conducting research. To collect the data, a self-administered online questionnaire was designed with a mix of list questions, category questions and six-point Likert-scales. The latter were used as semantic differential rating scales. The background to using six-point scales was linked to the preference that respondents choose between positive or negative ratings and may not be neutral as when using a five-point scale.

The author used the professional tool of www.onlineumfragen.com to conduct the research. By using a professional tool, it was ensured that all questions were easy to read, colour and font sizes were appropriate and that the format was comfortable to read (Saunders et al., 2009). The author chose a warm-pastel yellow as secondary colour to the white background, as this tends to generate slightly more responses than cool colours (Edwards et al., 2002). The online tool is designed to keep the participant focused and active, as only one question is shown at a time. In having to save each question after giving the answer, data losses are prevented in case the participant aborts the survey in the middle. Screenshots of the whole questionnaire may be found in Appendix 1.

The questions themselves were created to be unambiguous and understandable in a clear manner, so that respondents may understand them completely. Another advantage of an online survey is that respondents have as much time as they need and are able to answer the questionnaire in their comfortable home environment. They are able to link and complete it according to their personal schedule (Bryman and Bell, 2007). In order to minimize possible disadvantages of the method, several actions were taken. First, if there was any problem with a respondent understanding a question, the author could be contacted by E-Mail via an allocated button during every stage of the survey. In addition, a cover letter (Appendix 2.) that explained the aims of the study and ensured the anonymity of the participant was attached to the survey.

3.2.2 Tool Pilot Phase

Research methods literature points out the importance and essentiality of piloting the research tool before the actual data collection process. Bell (2005) points out that the researcher may gain security about the success of the tool by piloting it. Such a pre-test could lead to improvement of the questionnaire, ensuring that respondents may easily answer the questions without having queries (Saunders et al., 2009; Allen et al., 2008). Bryman and Bell (2007) state that the individuals testing the survey should not be members of the sample that would be employed in the full study, as it would affect the representativeness of any subsequent sample. In accordance, the questionnaire had been tested among ten non-Edinburgh Napier University students. The piloting resulted in some minor changes in the survey wording through responses and comments of the pre-test participants. Furthermore, one question had been left out. The author timed the participants, ensuring that the questionnaire could be completed in less than five minutes, which is a crucial factor to obtaining a sufficient number of completes. After this test, the author was sure that the instructions were suitable (Saunders et al., 2009), that the design of the questionnaire was beneficial (Iarossi, 2006) and that the wording was correct and clear (Biemer and Lyberg, 2003).

3.3 Sample Structure

With respect to the time measures and the limited financial resources of these studies, the convenience sampling method is used. This approach (Black, 2010) usually involves elements that are readily available, nearby and willing to participate in the research. Davies (2007) argues that convenience sample is appropriate for student research projects despite its limitations. Even though this approach may cause bias and there are issues regarding generalisation, it gives the opportunity to generate insights on the researched topic and aims (Bryman and Bell, 2007).

In the available case, the sample consisted of the student body of Edinburgh Napier University (ENU) and private contacts of the author to UK students. The participants had been invited (Appendix 2.) via the ENU E-Mail system. The message sent contained a direct link to the online survey, to ensure that the participation is as convenient as possible. As an incentive for participation, it was stated that a donation to World Vision would be made for every fully completed questionnaire. The survey had been available for the participants for one week from Monday, the 4th of July 2011 until Sunday, the 10th of July 2011. As a result, 541 respondents opened the survey, 379 answered at least one question and 355 respondents completed the full questionnaire. Compared to the required minimum response rate of 80, an actual feedback consisting of N = 355 completes may be seen as a successful research outcome.

3.4 Analysis

The data analysis will be carried out using the SPSS statistics program, Version 18 (Carver and Nash, 2009). Allen and Bennett (2010) present a decision tree as an aid to which statistical tests may be carried out using different data sets or samples. Within six steps, the appropriate test may be identified. Firstly, the number of dependent variables (DV) has to be taken into consideration, which in the present case was one per question. Second, the analyst may choose between scale, ordinal and nominal data. Since the answers of the questionnaire were designed to produce nominal data as an outcome, apart from the Likert scale questions, the latter will be chosen to analyse the dataset. Third, the number of independent variables (IV) is given as "one". Fourth, the analyst may choose the number of samples from one to three. To display whether some answers have a higher frequency then others, the χ^2 test for goodness of fit will be chosen. To compare two IVs, the χ^2 test of contingencies will be conducted. A graphical output to assess the results of the questionnaire will be provided by frequency analysis. The results to the Likert scale questions will be analysed using descriptive statistics.

3.5 Limitations

Adams et al. (2007) highlight that a study of high quality must be reliable, valid and generalizable. But as the test-retest and the split-half (Bryman and Bell, 2007) methods are too time consuming for this type of research, the author focussed on making this study replicable, which ensures reliability in order to cope with the explained limitations. The explanation of the approach, sampling and instrument may lead anyone who wishes to repeat the work in the future. Blaxter et al. (2006) point out that the pilot phase of the research tool is very significant for confirming its reliability and validity, as this phase confirms that the tool is measuring what it is supposed to measure, making it more valid.

Adams et al. (2007) highlight the importance of generalizability, as it helps to broaden the existing research in a field. Therefore the sample has to be representative to the whole population (Bryman and Bell, 2007). This aspect might be difficult to fulfil, as the research had been undertaken within a student segment living in the UK, but possibly with a wide range of personal and cultural origins. To generate a deeper understanding of the topic, the research might be conduced to other age and occupational groups in future. The field of PR is quite broad; therefore future studies might be focussing on certain instruments for more detailed findings. As the work of Hauss (1993) and Beth (1994) displayed, PR actions may not be easily measured and often require deeper company information. Therefore, this study gives implications on the perception of airline PR measures within the student segment, but when looking at distinct companies or customer groups, further research might be considered.

This chapter provided the reader with detailed information on the research process, explaining the Hypotheses, the research tool, the sample used, and the limitations of this study. With a regard to ethics, the author wrote this sturdy in respect of the ethical requirements of Edinburgh Napier University. The author had not any intention to manipulate any findings or deceive the study participants in order to take personal advantage.

4. Findings & Discussion

Following the deduction process introduced in chapter 3., this chapter will present the findings of the primary research. Considering the results, the hypotheses shown in 3.1 will be either confirmed or rejected. Lastly, this chapter will provide a critical review of the theory provided in chapter 2., the literature review.

4.1 Respondent Profile

The adjacent table 4.1.1 provides a brief profile of the sample structure, provided by descriptive statistics. The results show that the majority of respondents were female (62.8%). Furthermore, the respondents had been allocated to three age groups, 18 – 24 (47.3%), 25 – 29 (30.4%) and older than 30 years (22.3%). Considering the survey had been carried out among students, the age distribution represents the targeted population well.

		No of Respondents	**Percentage %**
Gender	Male	132	37.2
	Female	223	62.8
Age	18 - 24	168	47.3
	25 - 29	108	30.4
	> 30	79	22.3
Paid Job	Yes	221	62.4
	No	133	37.6
Annual Flights	0 - 2 times	186	49.1
	4 - 6 times	109	28.8
	> 6 times	84	22.2

Fig. 4.1.1: Sample Structure

In addition, 62.4% of the students work on a paid job beside their studies, implying that this group has a higher disposable income than the non-working students. Half of the respondents just tend to fly 0 – 2 times a year, whereas 28.8% fly between four and six times a year. Surprisingly, the sample contained a quite strong number of frequent flyers (22.2%), which fly more than six times annually.

4.2 Findings

The outcome of the primary research will be analysed according to the research aims introduced in chapter 1.3. Additional information to the presented graphs, like the n of the respondents to each variable, may be found in Appendix 3., which displays the conducted analysis as a whole.

Surprisingly, the vast majority (85.4%) of the respondents did fly with a budget airline in the past. This high percentage points out the importance LCCs have on the decision of the means of transport in the student segment. Furthermore, over three-fourths (78.1%) of the respondents tend to fly short-haul or intra-European, which is the operating ground of LCCs. Lastly, Fig. 4.2.1 shows that the two most frequently used airlines are RA and EJ, only followed up by Lufthansa as a traditional carrier in the third place.

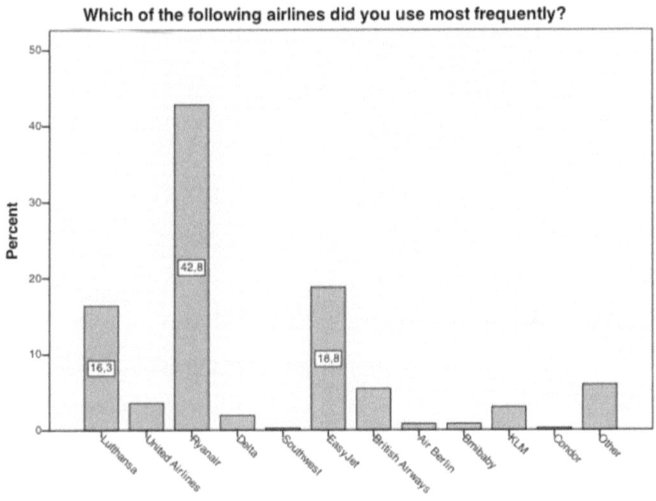

Fig. 4.2.1: Most Frequently used Airlines

Fig. 4.2.2 underscores the attitudes the respondents have towards LCCs. Almost half of them (47.8%) think that LCCs offer them a lower service quality, but it may be assumed that most of the travellers put up with this disadvantage, as they expect good value for money (31.1%) while flying with a budget airline. It is this trade off between low service and price that makes travellers think that LCCs are a good choice for short-haul flights (15%).

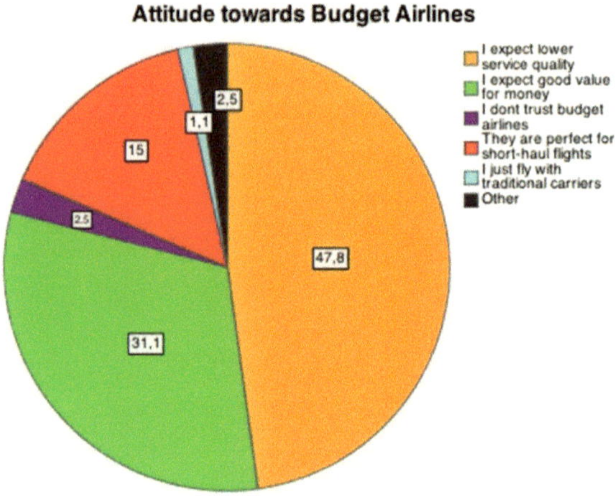

Fig. 4.2.2: Opinions on LCCs

A Pearson's chi-square test of contingencies (with $\alpha = .05$) was used to evaluate whether travellers have a tendency to use budget airlines the more often they fly. The chi-square test was statistically significant, χ^2 (1, $N = 377$) = 19.5, $p < .001$, $\Phi = .23$ (Appendix 3.3.1). It may be concluded that the more frequently a person travels, the more likely budget airlines to be used.

In addition to this, a Pearson's chi-square test (with $\alpha = .05$) had been done to assess if frequent flyers are more likely to be members of an airline loyalty scheme. The test, with χ^2 (1, $N = 354$) = 38.4, $p < .001$, $\Phi = .33$ (Appendix 3.3.1) showed that the respondents generally were not members of a loyalty scheme, but that they were more likely to be a member when they are flying up to six times a year and therefore more frequently.

4.2.1 PR and Decision Making

This chapter corresponds to the influence of PR on the consumer decision-making process. The descriptive analysis (Appendix 3.2) shows that:

H_1 Ticket price is the most crucial factor for decision-making

May be strongly confirmed. The respondents ($N = 363$) answered the six-point Likert scale on price importance with a mean of 1.51 and a low standard deviation of .82, meaning that the price of the ticket is very important to them. This corresponds to the findings of Ruiz-Mafé et al. (2009) and Dolnicar et al. (2011). The results are in contrast of the findings of Gallarza and Saura (2006) who mention that price is not that important within the student segment.

H_2 helps to evaluate the point of purchase of an airline ticket, or the tool used for booking:

H_2 Price comparison websites are used more often then company websites

Figure 4.2.1.1 shows that the most commonly used tools are the airline's homepage (39.9%) and OTAs (32.7%). In light of these results, H_2 may be rejected. But these outcomes confirm the strong Internet relation of the business, as Euromonitor International (2010) shows. The findings support the results of Koo et al. (2011) stating that the airline's own website is the major booking tool (39.9%), and that companies shall run a multi-channel strategy to stay competitive.

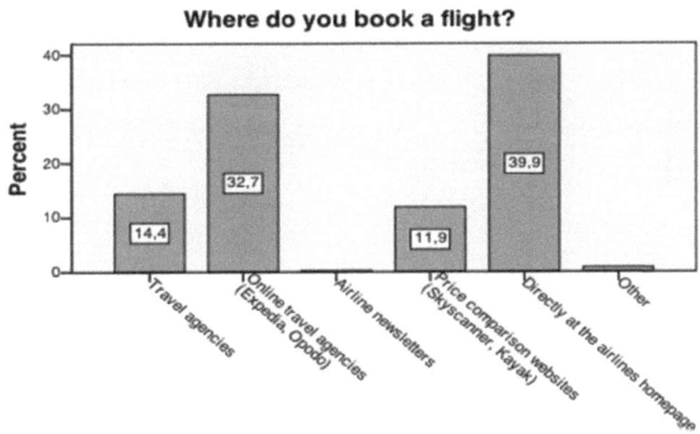

Fig. 4.2.1.1: Booking Tools Frequency

Figure 4.2.1.2 demonstrates the choice of the different booking tools in light of the distinctive flights-per-year groups. There is a clear trend that travellers with a higher annual flight frequency are less likely to book with OTAs. The overall most commonly used tool is the airline's homepage.

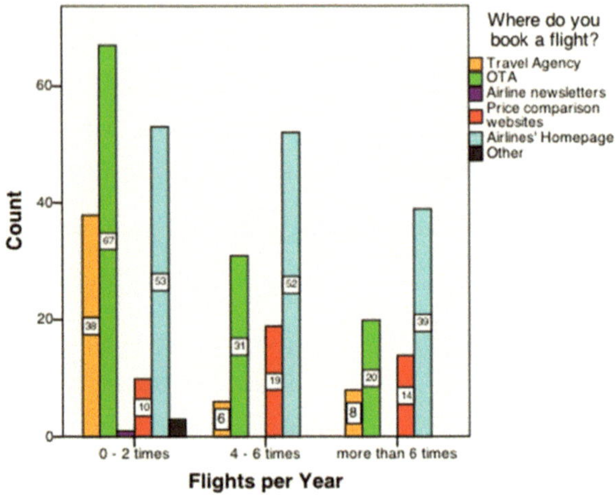

Fig. 4.2.1.2: Booking Tools by Flight Group

A chi-square test for goodness of fit (with $\alpha = .05$) was used to assess whether some booking tools were preferred over the other (Appendix 3.3.2). Of the five options, the airline's homepage ($N = 144$) and OTAs ($N = 118$) were reported with a greater frequency than others. The chi-square test was statistically significant, χ^2 (5, $N = 361$) = 290.906, $p < .0001$.

4.2.2 PR as a Communication Tool

The evaluation of H_3 helps to understand which PR measures are recognized by the student segment, and therefore have an impact on that group:

H_3 Most of airlines' PR measures are unrecognized by students

The results (Fig. 4.2.2.1) show that the two most frequently recognized PR measures are the company's website (34.4%) and online newsletters (22.6%). This is an interesting finding, as it once more supports the importance of the Internet in today's communication environment. Classic communication tools such as TV ads or direct mail do not seem to catch the attention of the student target group any more. Therefore H_3 may be supported. In this context, the findings of Macleod (2010) are interesting, as he mentions that the online communication power is often in the hands of few.

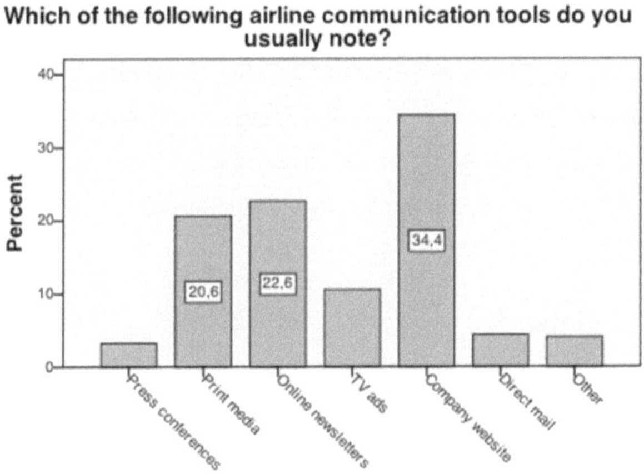

Fig. 4.2.2.1: PR Tool Recognition

Furthermore, a chi-square test for goodness of fit (with $\alpha = .05$) was used to assess whether some PR measures were more widely recognized over the other (Appendix 3.3.2). Of the six options, the company website ($N = 117$) and the online newsletters ($N = 77$) were reported with a greater frequency than others. The chi-square test was statistically significant, $\chi^2 (6, N = 340) = 202.624, p < .0001$.

4.2.3 PR Perception in the Student Segment

H_4 and H_5 contribute to the importance and perception of PR measures within the student segment:

H_4 Intensive advertising is perccived as disturbing

On a six-point Likert scale, the respondents answered with a mean of 4.94 and a standard deviation of 1.454 (Appendix 3.2), that they would rather not be interested in a weekly airline newsletter. Along with the findings from the previous chapter, which points out that e-mails are a PR Tool with a very good recognition, this may lead to the assumption that the respondents do use online newsletters, but in a selective manner, which corresponds to their interests. Bearing in mind that even a weekly newsletter could be perceived as disturbing, H_4 is supported.

H_5 PR measures are rather accepted when they are entertaining

To assess the link between corporate communication and entertainment, the respondents answered a six-point Likert scale question whether they would be more likely to buy a product if the corporate communication is entertaining or not. With a mean of 3.7 and a standard deviation of 1.544 (Appendix 3.2), the answer that entertaining corporate communication would not have a significant impact that could influence the purchase decision, meaning H_5 is rejected.

4.2.4 Marketing of Services

H_6 and H_7 give indications on the marketing of services, mainly related to the online environment of the airline business:

H_6 The student consumer will favour online bookings

Figure 4.2.1.1 signifies which tool the respondents use to book their flights. While grouping the internet-based possibilities, the outcome of 84.5% clearly displays that the student segment tends to prefer online bookings and H_6 is therefore supported. A Pearson's chi-square test of contingencies (with $\alpha = .05$) was used to evaluate what the traveller values, and if there are differences in values the more often a respondent flies in a year. The chi-square test was statistically significant, χ^2 (1, $N = 360$) = 22.87, $p < .001$, $\Phi = .25$ (Appendix 3.3.1). The test shows (Fig. 4.2.4.1) that on-board service is valued most, but as the number of flights per year increases, online check-in and online booking grow in importance.

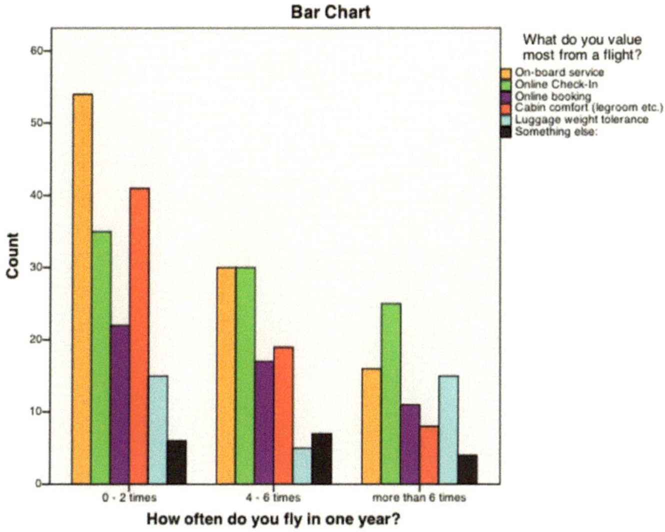

Fig. 4.2.4.1: Service Value by Flight Group

H_7 Airline newsletters trigger booking decisions

As mentioned in 4.2.2, newsletters are the second most recognized communication tool (22.6%) after the airline's website. Regarding this percentage, it is highly likely that newsletters trigger booking decisions and that H_7 is supported. But as described in 4.2.3, newsletters do not seem to be very popular among the respondents. It might be beneficial for airlines to send out newsletters with a lower frequency -e.g. once a month- to not be perceived as disturbing.

4.2.5 Airline Selection Factors

H_8 and H_9 help to generate an understanding of the factors the customer takes into account when selecting an airline:

H_8 Service is less relevant than price

As we could see in Fig. 4.2.2, the respondents expect a lower service quality when travelling with budget airlines, which is well supported by Chiou and Chen (2010). In addition, they assume a good value for money ratio, which corresponds to the findings of Doganis (2006). Chapter 4.2.1 points out the importance of price as a decision factor. Based on these two previous analyses, H_8 might be supported in the student segment with a regard to LCCs. Fig. 4.2.5.1 shows which services are important to the consumers, with on-board service and online check-in evolving to be the most crucial factors.

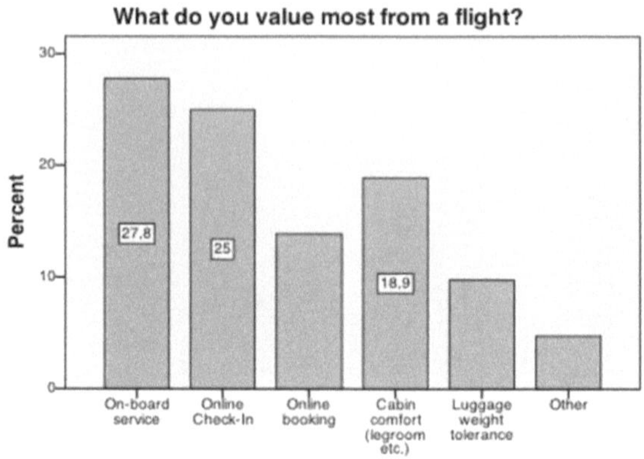

Fig. 4.2.5.1: Service Value Frequencies

H_9 The reputation of an airline is rather unimportant for students

On a six-point Likert scale, the respondents answered with a mean of 2.41 and a standard deviation of 1.164 (Appendix 3.2) if the reputation of an airline is important to them. Considering the mean of 2.41, this is the case and H_9 must be rejected in consequence. This points out the importance of branding within PR, as it is a PR responsibility to form a picture of the company in the consumers' minds through a shared vision (Tench and Yeomans, 2009).

4.3 Summary of Findings

The research of this paper is following the deduction process, which supports the overall coherence. After having introduced the research aims in 1.3, the hypotheses were developed (3.1) to support those aims. The findings of the primary research were then presented in 4.2, leading to conclusions in the subsequent chapter.

The analysis chapter brought up interesting findings, which will be summed up subsequently. The vast majority (85.4%) of the respondents did fly with a budget airline in the past, using RA and EJ as the most frequent carriers. The major attitude (47.8%) towards LCCs is that they offer a lower service quality, but good value for money (31.1%). Furthermore, price is the most crucial decision factor for travelling students, who mainly book directly at the airline's homepage.

The research shows that the two most frequently recognized PR measures are the company's website (34.4%) and online newsletters (22.6%). This is a remarkable finding, as it once more supports the importance of the Internet in today's communication environment. It is important to keep the advertising frequency low, as too much advertising is perceived as disturbing. However entertaining advertising does not seem to have positive impact on purchase decisions.

There is a clear trend towards online bookings and services. Online newsletters lead to bookings through their informational content, but should be used carefully to avoid information overflow. Price seems to be valued more than the quality of service, at least in the student segment. Beside all price-related issues, the reputation of an airline is important to most of the students, which supports the importance of branding and public communications in order to achieve a reliable picture in consumers' minds.

5. Conclusion & Research Implications

This chapter will provide the reader with the conclusions drawn from the findings of the previously introduced results of the primary research process. The intention is the development of practical implications, which may be valuable for PR, marketing and airline professionals. In addition, the author will discuss the limitations of this paper, which will be closely linked to implications on further research projects. Chapter 1.3 introduced the aims of this paper, with the overall goal being to generate an understanding of how PR are currently used as a communication tool within the UK budget airline industry, and how the student segment responds to these measures. Along this overall aim, a set of nine hypotheses had been developed and evaluated. Subsequently, the author will link aims, hypotheses and findings to conclude the previous work.

With regards to decision-making, H_1 was clearly supported, claiming that price is the most crucial factor to trigger the booking decision. This implies that LCCs identified a gap in the airline market and that the low-price strategy is a successful one, specifically in times of economic downswing. Low fares are therefore a powerful communication tool. They allow the attraction of a wide range of customers without stressing the advertising budget to a greater extent, as savvy consumers will seek the best price, especially in the student segment, which is highly internet-affine. The importance of an appropriate web-presence had been tested with H_2, which suggested that price comparison websites would be used more often than airline's homepages. As this hypothesis had been rejected, the need for a suitable corporate website emerges, as this is the most commonly used tool for online bookings. Partnerships involving OTAs may still be seen as favourable, as many participants do their bookings via this distribution channel. This could mean an additional source of revenue, especially for RA and EJ, who sell their online tickets exclusively via their own corporate web portals. Combining both the corporate homepage and OTA partnerships may lead to an increase in brand awareness and result in improved market share of the airline.

The conducted research showed that there is a shift in the use of advertising and communication tools. H_3 was supported, assuming that most of airlines' PR measures are unrecognized by students. Namely, classical corporate communication channels such as TV ads or direct mail are almost unrecognized, whereas the airlines' website is the most recognized communication channel. Knowing this, airline managers might use other print media -which still draws customer attention- to support the online presence. Furthermore, a high ranking in search engines and enhanced usability, as well as a facilitation of the content for visually impaired individuals, is of importance.

On one hand, communication through E-Mail offers advantages to marketing professionals, as it is convenient and comparably cost effective, but H_4 proves, that companies have to use this tool wisely and selectively, as intense advertising is perceived as disturbing. Key to successful E-Mail communication may be a low frequency of E-Mails per month, paired with valuable content or offers for the customer, as the results had shown that E-Mails are widely recognized. Within airline communication, professionals have to bear in mind that trust plays an important role when approaching customers. Therefore H_5 had been rejected, as is presumed that PR measures are rather accepted when they are entertaining. In the opinion of the author, the "entertainment-factor" of an ad or campaign should be majorly linked to the nature of the business or advertised product. Viral campaigns may be highly successful using humorous content, but might not be the appropriate tool for the trust-related business of air transportation.

As previously stated, the process of seeking and booking a flight is vastly undertaken online, which supported H_6. This has an impact on the marketing of services, as once more the attention is shifted from classical distribution channels such as a TA to the corporate website or OTAs. As the use of the Internet will increase in the future, communication professionals may focus on enhanced convenience of the online processes. This could include the offer of a variety of payment methods or the issue of an application for smartphone devices.

The research showed that print media still has its place in the current advertising and corporate communication environment, and it may be assumed that it will never entirely disappear, but it has been indicated that E-Mails do trigger booking decisions to a great extent. They will be the corporate communication tools of the future, as they are convenient to distribute and cost efficient. H_7 evaluated the relation of E-Mails and booking decisions, and is consequently supported. Along with the facts mentioned before, airlines need to recognize and use the chances offered by communication through social media. Networks as Facebook, Twitter or Google+ create new options for advertising and give space for corporate representation, which reaches the customer in a very direct manner. Using these networks requires fast adaption to change and a clear understanding of the targeted customer base. If airlines can keep up with the speed of development, they gain a highly efficient mass communication tool, which may be maintained with comparable low cost and effort. Furthermore, the use of social media may be a chance for companies to collect customer feedback, helping them to respond better to customer needs and therewith enhance customer satisfaction.

Concerning the selection factors and stimuli, which lead the student consumer to a booking decision, it may be said that most of the customers have a good understanding of what to expect when choosing a budget airline. As H_8 evaluated, service is indeed less relevant than price within the student segment. Given this fact, it may be derived that the current strategy of LCCs-offering good value for money- is sustainably successful. To ensure future growth of the business, LCCs may also apply their concept to long-haul routes, a segment that is still mainly dominated by traditional carriers. Whether budget airline or traditional carrier, the reputation of an airline is important to the student customer. H_9 predicted the opposite, and thus had been rejected. This circumstance displays the weight marketing and communication professionals should put on branding and positioning of their airline, as positive brand awareness leads to better recognition of the communication tools and results in higher booking rates.

All in all, PR efforts play a significant role in supporting the achievement of sales goals and sustainable financial success. To reach a broad audience, airlines might rely on a multi-channel communication strategy with a focus on online tools, which are especially appreciated by the researched student segment. Offering good value for money is the right strategy, if long-term profitability is ensured. Marketers need to carefully evaluate the frequency of their communication, as different customer segments will have different perceptions of ads and communication measures. Lastly, service value should be created where it is inexpensive to implement and easy to maintain -at the companies' websites- to stimulate booking decisions and to be ahead of competition.

As previously outlined in chapter 3.5, there are certain limitations that affect this paper. Although the number of participants was sufficient for a student project, there is room for future research to repeat the findings within a larger group of respondents. Furthermore it might be interesting to interview participants of different occupational groups to evaluate the differences and similarities of their answers. With a regard to the sample it would have been helpful if all the students were born in the UK, but the nature of convenience sampling within the very international student base of ENU lead to a national variety of respondents. The use and perception of E-Mail communication especially would be an interesting field of further research, as it is a highly recognized tool, but if used too often, it may be perceived as disturbing. Managers may benefit from knowing what would be the "ideal" frequency of E-Mail messaging, also related to age or occupational groups.

As the literature review pointed out, there is no general way to measure the impact of PR actions. The success of advertising campaigns might be assessed with a regard to sales numbers over a certain amount of time, but ideally the impact of certain communication tools may be evaluated with research panels, which requires both temporal and monetary resources.

Given these requirements, an appraisal of the differences in communication between LCCs and traditional carriers might contribute to the scientific knowledge in this field.

Appendices

1. Survey Screenshots

Question 1

How often do you fly in one year?

- 0 - 2 times
- 4 - 6 times
- more than 6 times

Save - next question!

Question 2

Are you rather flying to:

- European destinations?
- Destinations outside Europe?

Save - next question!

Question 3

Did you ever fly with a budget airline, e.g. Ryanair or easyJet?

- Yes
- No

Save - next question!

Question 4

Which of the following airlines did you use most frequently?

Multiple answers possible - Maximum 4 answers

- ☐ Lufthansa
- ☐ United Airlines
- ☐ Ryanair
- ☐ Delta
- ☐ Southwest
- ☐ EasyJet
- ☐ British Airways
- ☐ Air Berlin
- ☐ Bmibaby
- ☐ KLM
- ☐ Condor
- ☐ Other:

Further remarks regarding this question:

Save - next question!

Question 5

Which two of the following options describe your attitude towards budget airlines?

Multiple answers possible - Maximum 2 answers

- ☐ I expect lower service quality
- ☐ I expect good value for money
- ☐ I don't trust budget airlines
- ☐ They are perfect for short-haul flights
- ☐ I just fly with traditional carriers
- ☐ I think this:

Further remarks regarding this question:

Save - next question!

Question 6

What do you value most from a flight?

Multiple answers possible

- ☐ On-board service
- ☐ Online Check-In
- ☐ Online booking
- ☐ Cabin comfort (legroom etc.)
- ☐ Luggage weight tolerance
- ☐ Something else:

Further remarks regarding this question:

Save - next question!

Question 7

How important is the price of the ticket for you?

Very important ○ ○ ○ ○ ○ ○ Not important

Save - next question!

Question 8

Where do you book a flight?

Multiple answers possible

- ☐ Travel agencies
- ☐ Online travel agencies (Expedia, Opodo)
- ☐ Airline newsletters
- ☐ Price comparison websites (Skyscanner, Kayak, Swoodoo)
- ☐ Directly at the airline's homepage
- ☐ Somewhere else:

Further remarks regarding this question:

Save - next question!

Question 9

Which of the following airline communication tools do you usually note?

Multiple answers possible

- ☐ Press conferences
- ☐ Print media
- ☐ Online newsletters
- ☐ TV ads
- ☐ Company website
- ☐ Direct mail
- ☐ Other:

Further remarks regarding this question:

Save - next question!

Question 10

Would you be interested in a weekly airline Newsletter?

Very interested ○ ○ ○ ○ ○ ○ Not interested

Save - next question!

Question 11

Are you more likely to purchase a product, if the corporate communication is entertaining?

I strongly agree ○ ○ ○ ○ ○ ○ I disagree

Save - next question!

Question 12

The reputation of an airline for me is

Very important ○ ○ ○ ○ ○ ○ Not important

Save - next question!

Question 13

Are you member of an airline loyalty program?

○ Yes
○ No

Save - next question!

Question 14

Do you have a paid job beside your studies?

- ◯ Yes
- ◯ No

Save - next question!

Question 15

How old are you?

- ◯ 18 - 24
- ◯ 25 - 29
- ◯ older than 30

Save - next question!

Question 16

Which gender are you?

- ◯ Female
- ◯ Male

Save - next question!

2. Invitation E-Mail and Survey Start Page

Dear fellow student,

I am participating the postgraduate program "International Marketing with Tourism & Events". To complete my studies, I am currently writing my master's study about the "Impact of PR as a Communication Tool of U.K. Budget Airlines". Therefore I would be grateful if you could support my work by following the adjacent link to fill out a five-minute survey.

There will be a donation to World Vision for every fully completed survey.

Thank you for your help!

With best regards

Matthias Schimmel
4/7 Robertson Gait
EH11 1HJ Edinburgh

Student of the program:

"MSc International Marketing with Tourism & Events", Edinburgh Napier University

If you have any further questions, please contact me under this E-mail address:

10016520@live.napier.ac.uk

Supervisor:
Professor Graeme Drummond
Senior Lecturer and Teaching Fellow
School of Marketing, Tourism & Languages
Edinburgh Napier University

Dear fellow student,

With your participation you help to generate new findings about how corporate communication of budget airlines may influence the student segment. All data is collected anonymously and will only be used as a basis for my MSc study, the “Impact of PR as a Communication Tool of U.K. Budget Airlines”.

There will be a donation to World Vision for every fully completed survey.

With best regards

Matthias Schimmel
4/7 Robertson Gait
EH11 1HJ Edinburgh

Student of the program:
"MSc International Marketing with Tourism & Events", Edinburgh Napier University

If you have any further questions, please contact me under this E-mail address:

10016520@live.napier.ac.uk

Supervisor:

Professor Graeme Drummond
Senior Lecturer and Teaching Fellow
School of Marketing, Tourism & Languages
Edinburgh Napier University

3. Statistical Analysis

3.1 Frequency Distributions

Statistics

How often do you fly in one year?

N	Valid	379
	Missing	0

How often do you fly in one year?

		Frequency	Percent	Valid Percent	Cumulative Percent
Valid	0 - 2 times	186	49,1	49,1	49,1
	4 - 6 times	109	28,8	28,8	77,8
	more than 6 times	84	22,2	22,2	100,0
	Total	379	100,0	100,0	

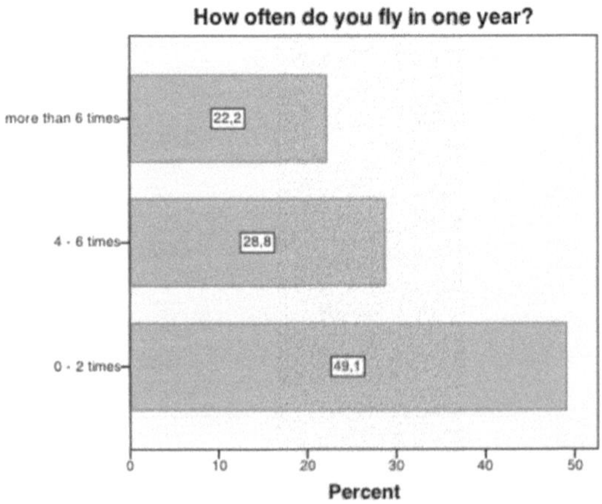

Statistics

Are you rather flying to:

N	Valid	379
	Missing	0

Are you rather flying to:

		Frequency	Percent	Valid Percent	Cumulative Percent
Valid	European destinations?	296	78,1	78,1	78,1
	Destinations outside Europe?	83	21,9	21,9	100,0
	Total	379	100,0	100,0	

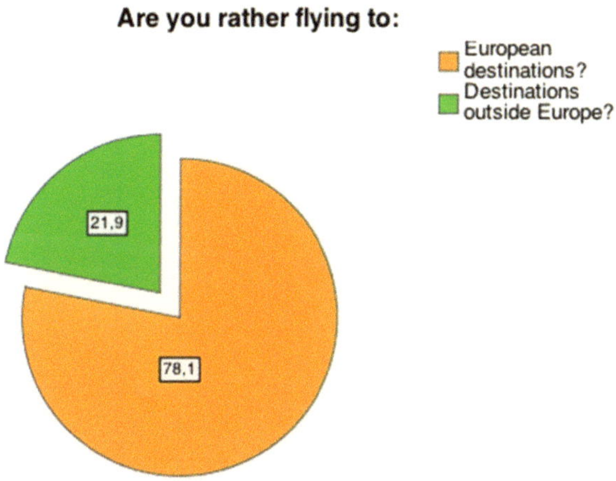

Statistics

Did you ever fly with a budget airline, e.g. Ryanair or easyJet?

N	Valid	377
	Missing	2

Did you ever fly with a budget airline, e.g. Ryanair or easyJet?

		Frequency	Percent	Valid Percent	Cumulative Percent
Valid	Yes	322	85,0	85,4	85,4
	No	55	14,5	14,6	100,0
	Total	377	99,5	100,0	
Missing	System	2	,5		
Total		379	100,0		

Did you ever fly with a budget airline, e.g. Ryanair or easyJet?

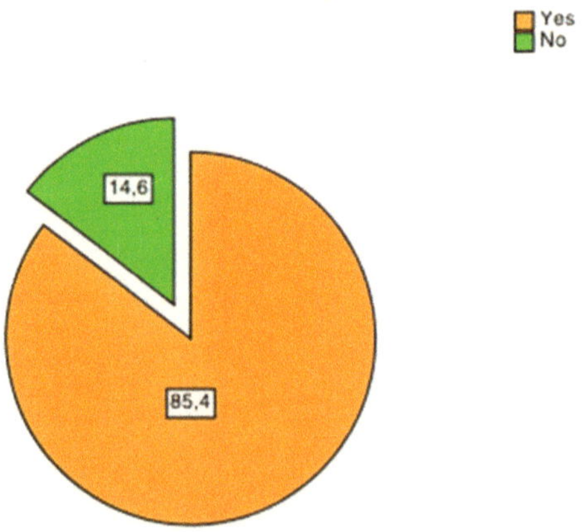

Which of the following airlines did you use most frequently?

		Frequency	Percent	Valid Percent	Cumulative Percent
Valid	Lufthansa	60	15,8	16,3	16,3
	United Airlines	13	3,4	3,5	19,9
	Ryanair	157	41,4	42,8	62,7
	Delta	7	1,8	1,9	64,6
	Southwest	1	,3	,3	64,9
	EasyJet	69	18,2	18,8	83,7
	British Airways	20	5,3	5,4	89,1
	Air Berlin	3	,8	,8	89,9
	Bmibaby	3	,8	,8	90,7
	KLM	11	2,9	3,0	93,7
	Condor	1	,3	,3	94,0
	Other:	22	5,8	6,0	100,0
	Total	367	96,8	100,0	
Missing	System	12	3,2		
Total		379	100,0		

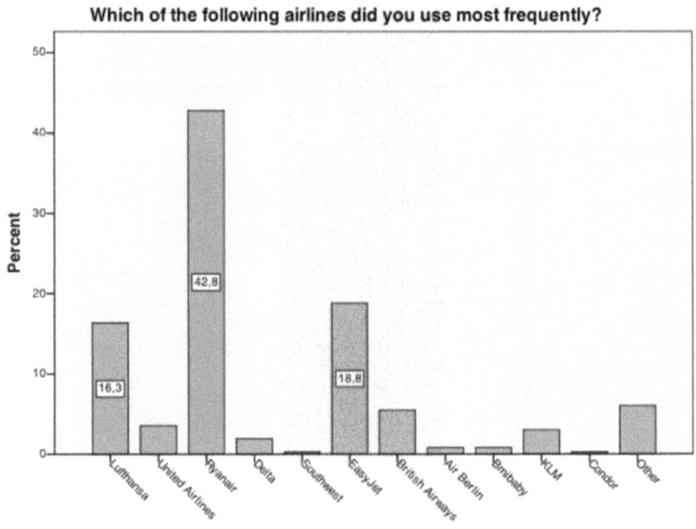

Statistics

Which two of the following options describe your attitude towards budget airlines?

N	Valid	366
	Missing	13

Which two of the following options describe your attitude towards budget airlines?

		Frequency	Percent	Valid Percent	Cumulative Percent
Valid	I expect lower service quality	175	46,2	47,8	47,8
	I expect good value for money	114	30,1	31,1	79,0
	I don't trust budget airlines	9	2,4	2,5	81,4
	They are perfect for short-haul flights	55	14,5	15,0	96,4
	I just fly with traditional carriers	4	1,1	1,1	97,5
	I think this:	9	2,4	2,5	100,0
	Total	366	96,6	100,0	
Missing	System	13	3,4		
Total		379	100,0		

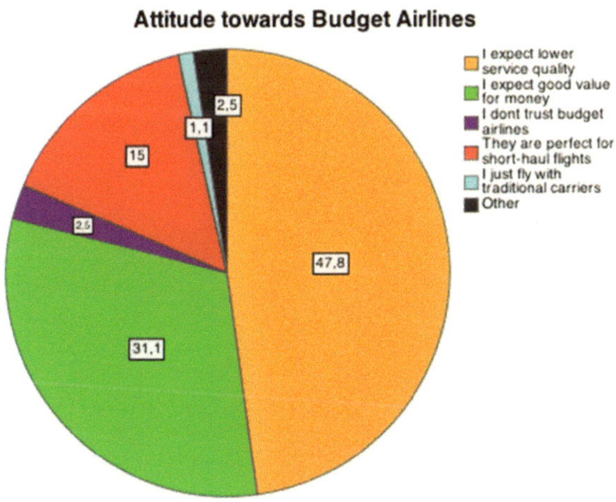

What do you value most from a flight?

		Frequency	Percent	Valid Percent	Cumulative Percent
Valid	On-board service	100	26,4	27,8	27,8
	Online Check-In	90	23,7	25,0	52,8
	Online booking	50	13,2	13,9	66,7
	Cabin comfort (legroom etc.)	68	17,9	18,9	85,6
	Luggage weight tolerance	35	9,2	9,7	95,3
	Something else:	17	4,5	4,7	100,0
	Total	360	95,0	100,0	
Missing	System	19	5,0		
Total		379	100,0		

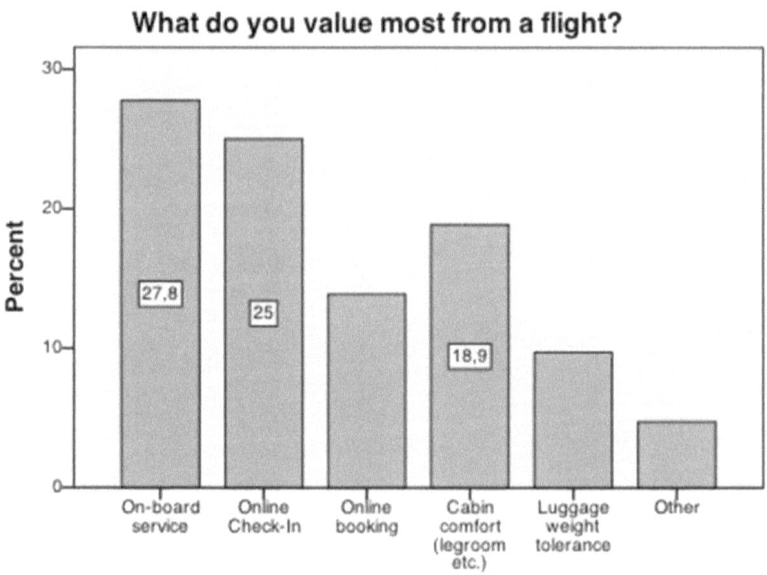

Statistics

Where do you book a flight?

N	Valid	361
	Missing	18

Where do you book a flight?

		Frequency	Percent	Valid Percent	Cumulative Percent
Valid	Travel agencies	52	13,7	14,4	14,4
	Online travel agencies (Expedia, Opodo)	118	31,1	32,7	47,1
	Airline newsletters	1	,3	,3	47,4
	Price comparison websites (Skyscanner, Kayak)	43	11,3	11,9	59,3
	Directly at the airlines homepage	144	38,0	39,9	99,2
	Other	3	,8	,8	100,0
	Total	361	95,3	100,0	
Missing	System	18	4,7		
Total		379	100,0		

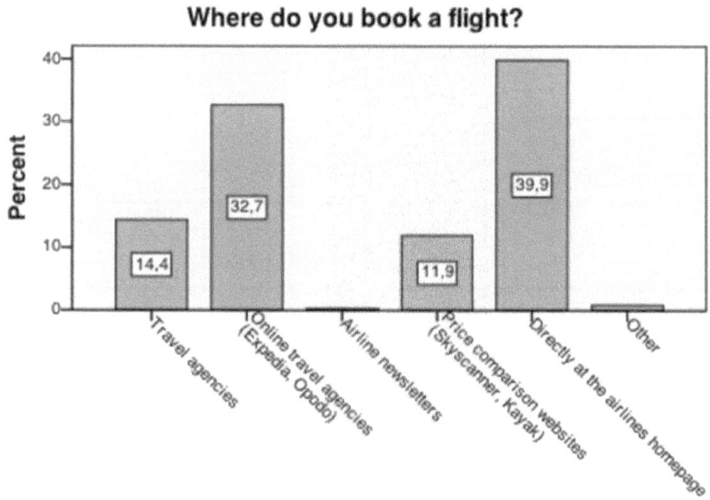

Statistics

Which of the following airline communication tools do you usually note?

N	Valid	340
	Missing	39

Which of the following airline communication tools do you usually note?

		Frequency	Percent	Valid Percent	Cumulative Percent
Valid	Press conferences	11	2,9	3,2	3,2
	Print media	70	18,5	20,6	23,8
	Online newsletters	77	20,3	22,6	46,5
	TV ads	36	9,5	10,6	57,1
	Company website	117	30,9	34,4	91,5
	Direct mail	15	4,0	4,4	95,9
	Other:	14	3,7	4,1	100,0
	Total	340	89,7	100,0	
Missing	System	39	10,3		
Total		379	100,0		

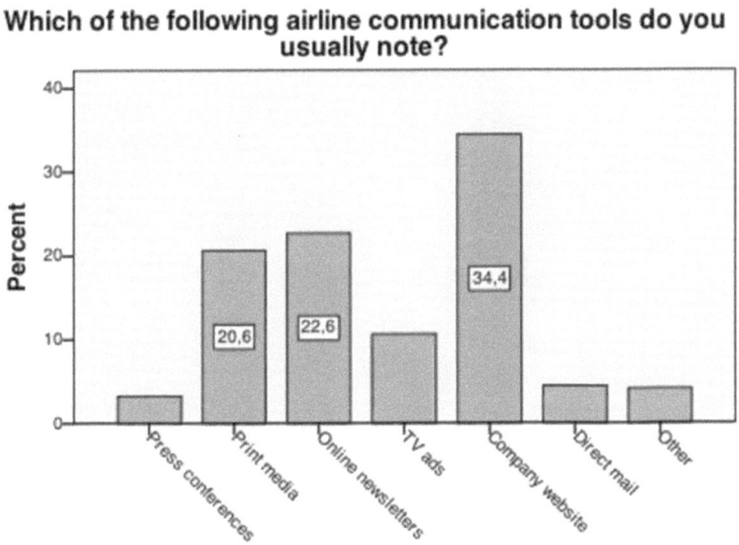

Statistics

Are you member of an airline loyalty program?

N	Valid	354
	Missing	25

Are you member of an airline loyalty program?

		Frequency	Percent	Valid Percent	Cumulative Percent
Valid	Yes	80	21,1	22,6	22,6
	No	274	72,3	77,4	100,0
	Total	354	93,4	100,0	
Missing	System	25	6,6		
Total		379	100,0		

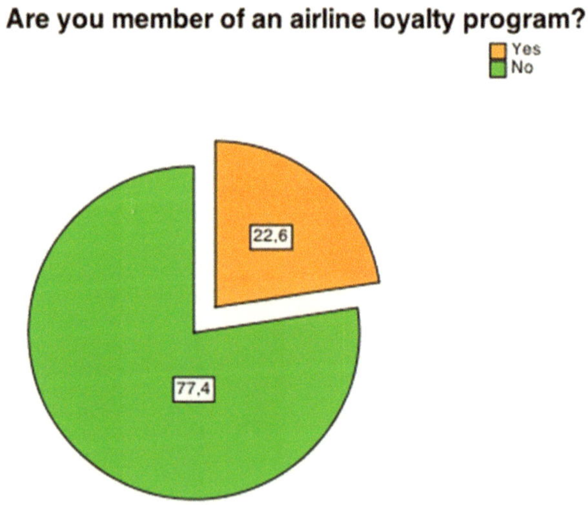

Statistics

Do you have a paid job beside your studies?

N	Valid	354
	Missing	25

Do you have a paid job beside your studies?

		Frequency	Percent	Valid Percent	Cumulative Percent
Valid	Yes	221	58,3	62,4	62,4
	No	133	35,1	37,6	100,0
	Total	354	93,4	100,0	
Missing	System	25	6,6		
Total		379	100,0		

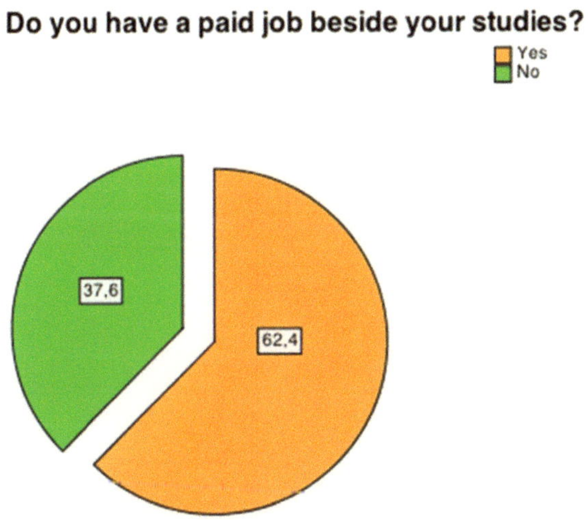

Statistics

How old are you?

N	Valid	355
	Missing	24

How old are you?

		Frequency	Percent	Valid Percent	Cumulative Percent
Valid	18 - 24	168	44,3	47,3	47,3
	25 - 29	108	28,5	30,4	77,7
	older than 30	79	20,8	22,3	100,0
	Total	355	93,7	100,0	
Missing	System	24	6,3		
Total		379	100,0		

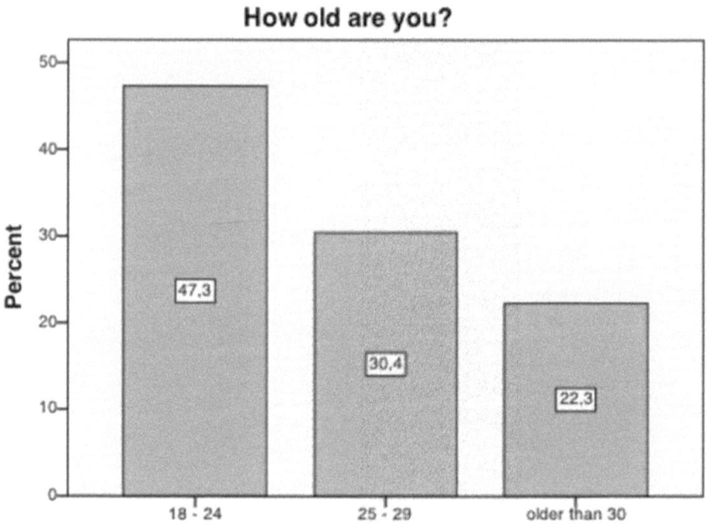

Statistics

Which gender are you?

N	Valid	355
	Missing	24

Which gender are you?

		Frequency	Percent	Valid Percent	Cumulative Percent
Valid	Female	223	58,8	62,8	62,8
	Male	132	34,8	37,2	100,0
	Total	355	93,7	100,0	
Missing	System	24	6,3		
Total		379	100,0		

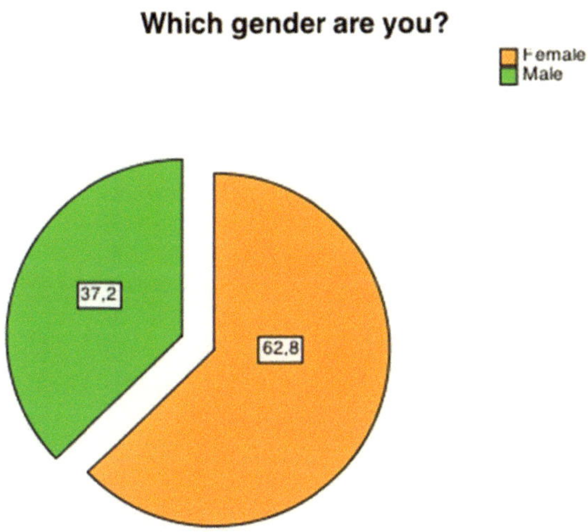

3.2 Descriptive Statistics

Descriptive Statistics

	N	Minimum	Maximum	Mean	Std. Deviation
How important is the price of the ticket for you?	363	1	6	1,51	,819
Would you be interested in a weekly airline Newsletter?	360	1	6	4,94	1,454
Are you more likely to purchase a product, if the corporate communication is entertaining?	357	1	6	3,70	1,544
The reputation of an airline for me is	357	1	6	2,41	1,164
Valid N (listwise)	356				

3.3 χ^2 Tests

3.3.1 χ^2 Contingencies

Case Processing Summary

	Cases					
	Valid		Missing		Total	
	N	Percent	N	Percent	N	Percent
How often do you fly in one year? * Where do you book a flight?	361	95,3%	18	4,7%	379	100,0%

How often do you fly in one year? * Where do you book a flight? Crosstabulation

			Where do you book a flight?						
			Travel agencies	Online travel agencies (Expedia, Opodo)	Airline newsletters	Price comparison websites (Skyscanner, Kayak)	Directly at the airlines homepage	Somewh ere else :	Total
How often do you fly in one year?	0 - 2 times	Count	38	67	1	10	53	3	172
		% within Where do you book a flight?	73,1%	56,8%	100,0%	23,3%	36,8%	100,0%	47,6%
	4 - 6 times	Count	6	31	0	19	52	0	108
		% within Where do you book a flight?	11,5%	26,3%	,0%	44,2%	36,1%	,0%	29,9%
	more than 6 times	Count	8	20	0	14	39	0	81
		% within Where do you book a flight?	15,4%	16,9%	,0%	32,6%	27,1%	,0%	22,4%
Total		Count	52	118	1	43	144	3	361
		% within Where do you book a flight?	100,0%	100,0%	100,0%	100,0%	100,0%	100,0%	100,0%

Chi-Square Tests

	Value	df	Asymp. Sig. (2-sided)
Pearson Chi-Square	39,694[a]	10	,000
Likelihood Ratio	42,976	10	,000
Linear-by-Linear Association	18,043	1	,000
N of Valid Cases	361		

a. 6 cells (33,3%) have expected count less than 5. The minimum expected count is ,22.

Symmetric Measures

		Value	Approx. Sig.
Nominal by Nominal	Phi	,332	,000
	Cramer's V	,234	,000
N of Valid Cases		361	

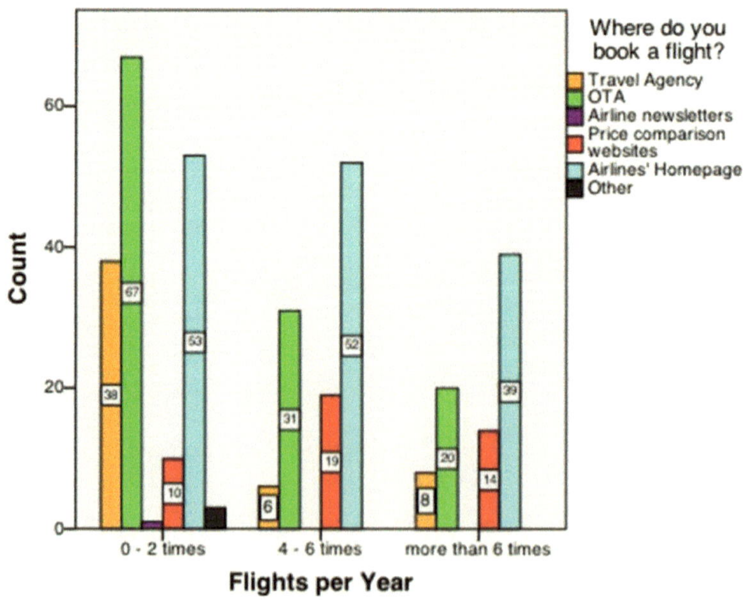

Case Processing Summary

	Cases				
	Valid		Missing		Total
	N	Percent	N	Percent	N
How often do you fly in one year? * Did you ever fly with a budget airline, e.g. Ryanair or easyJet?	377	99,5%	2	,5%	379

How often do you fly in one year? * Did you ever fly with a budget airline, e.g. Ryanair or easyJet? Crosstabulation

			Did you ever fly with a budget airline, e.g. Ryanair or easyJet?		
			Yes	No	Total
How often do you fly in one year?	0 - 2 times	Count	144	41	185
		% within How often do you fly in one year?	77,8%	22,2%	100,0%
	4 - 6 times	Count	97	12	109
		% within How often do you fly in one year?	89,0%	11,0%	100,0%
	more than 6 times	Count	81	2	83
		% within How often do you fly in one year?	97,6%	2,4%	100,0%
Total		Count	322	55	377
		% within How often do you fly in one year?	85,4%	14,6%	100,0%

Chi-Square Tests

	Value	df	Asymp. Sig. (2-sided)
Pearson Chi-Square	19,517[a]	2	,000
Likelihood Ratio	23,146	2	,000
Linear-by-Linear Association	19,369	1	,000
N of Valid Cases	377		

a. 0 cells (,0%) have expected count less than 5. The minimum expected count is 12,11.

Symmetric Measures

		Value	Approx. Sig.
Nominal by Nominal	Phi	,228	,000
	Cramer's V	,228	,000
N of Valid Cases		377	

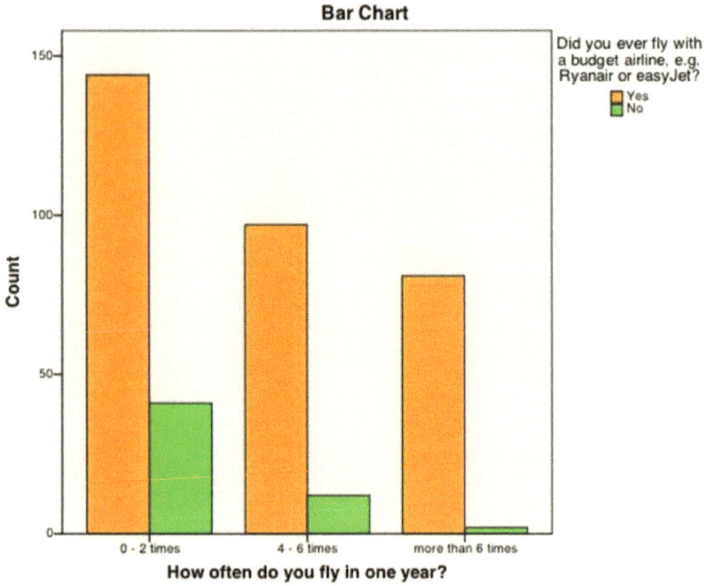

Case Processing Summary

	Cases				
	Valid		Missing		Total
	N	Percent	N	Percent	N
How often do you fly in one year? * Are you member of an airline loyalty program?	354	93,4%	25	6,6%	379

How often do you fly in one year? * Are you member of an airline loyalty program? Crosstabulation

			Are you member of an airline loyalty program?		
			Yes	No	Total
How often do you fly in one year?	0 - 2 times	Count	14	152	166
		% within How often do you fly in one year?	8,4%	91,6%	100,0%
	4 - 6 times	Count	33	74	107
		% within How often do you fly in one year?	30,8%	69,2%	100,0%
	more than 6 times	Count	33	48	81
		% within How often do you fly in one year?	40,7%	59,3%	100,0%
Total		Count	80	274	354
		% within How often do you fly in one year?	22,6%	77,4%	100,0%

Chi-Square Tests

	Value	df	Asymp. Sig. (2-sided)
Pearson Chi-Square	38,439[a]	2	,000
Likelihood Ratio	40,607	2	,000
Linear-by-Linear Association	36,731	1	,000
N of Valid Cases	354		

a. 0 cells (,0%) have expected count less than 5. The minimum expected count is 18,31.

Symmetric Measures

		Value	Approx. Sig.
Nominal by Nominal	Phi	,330	,000
	Cramer's V	,330	,000
N of Valid Cases		354	

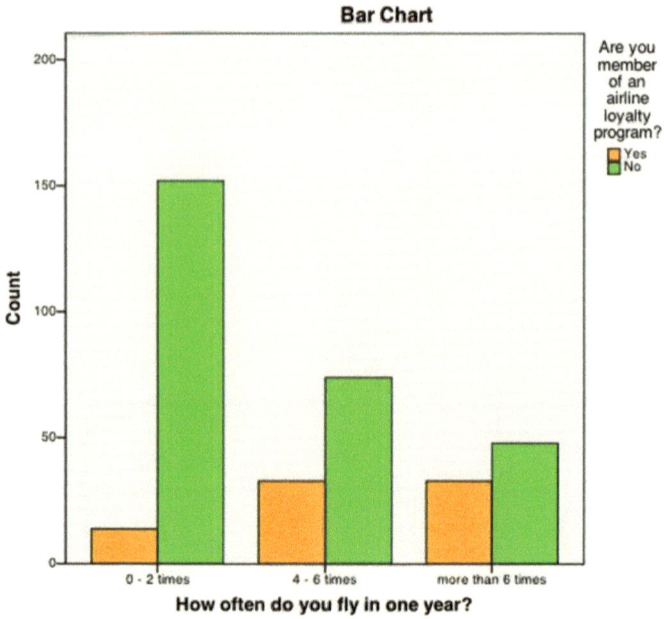

Case Processing Summary

	Cases					
	Valid		Missing		Total	
	N	Percent	N	Percent	N	Percent
How often do you fly in one year? * What do you value most from a flight?	360	95,0%	19	5,0%	379	100,0%

How often do you fly in one year? * What do you value most from a flight? Crosstabulation

		What do you value most from a flight?						
		On-board service	Online Check-In	Online booking	Cabin comfort (legroom etc.)	Luggage weight tolerance	Something else:	Total
How often do you fly in one year?	0 - 2 times	54 31,2%	35 20,2%	22 12,7%	41 23,7%	15 8,7%	6 3,5%	173 100,0%
	4 - 6 times	30 27,8%	30 27,8%	17 15,7%	19 17,6%	5 4,6%	7 6,5%	108 100,0%
	more than 6 times	16 20,3%	25 31,6%	11 13,9%	8 10,1%	15 19,0%	4 5,1%	79 100,0%
Total		100 27,8%	90 25,0%	50 13,9%	68 18,9%	35 9,7%	17 4,7%	360 100,0%

Chi-Square Tests

	Value	df	Asymp. Sig. (2-sided)
Pearson Chi-Square	22,869[a]	10	,011
Likelihood Ratio	22,652	10	,012
Linear-by-Linear Association	,816	1	,366
N of Valid Cases	360		

a. 1 cells (5,6%) have expected count less than 5. The minimum expected count is 3,73.

Symmetric Measures

		Value	Approx. Sig.
Nominal by Nominal	Phi	,252	,011
	Cramer's V	,178	,011
N of Valid Cases		360	

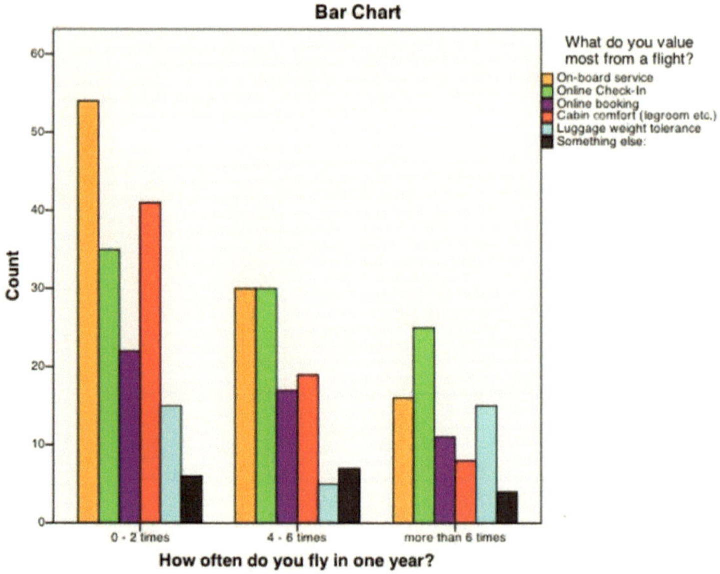

3.3.2 χ^2 Goodness of Fit

Where do you book a flight?

	Observed N	Expected N	Residual
Travel agencies	52	60,2	-8,2
Online travel agencies (Expedia, Opodo)	118	60,2	57,8
Airline newsletters	1	60,2	-59,2
Price comparison websites (Skyscanner, Kayak, Swoodoo)	43	60,2	-17,2
Directly at the airlines homepage	144	60,2	83,8
Somewhere else:	3	60,2	-57,2
Total	361		

Test Statistics

	Where do you book a flight?
Chi-square	290,906[a]
df	5
Asymp. Sig.	,000

a. 0 cells (,0%) have expected frequencies less than 5. The minimum expected cell frequency is 60,2.

Which of the following airline communication tools do you usually note?

	Observed N	Expected N	Residual
Press conferences	11	48,6	-37,6
Print media	70	48,6	21,4
Online newsletters	77	48,6	28,4
TV ads	36	48,6	-12,6
Company website	117	48,6	68,4
Direct mail	15	48,6	-33,6
Other:	14	48,6	-34,6
Total	340		

Test Statistics

	Which of the following airline communication tools do you usually note?
Chi-square	202,624[a]
df	6
Asymp. Sig.	,000

Test Statistics

	Which of the following airline communication tools do you usually note?
Chi-square	202,624[a]
df	6
Asymp. Sig.	,000

a. 0 cells (,0%) have expected frequencies less than 5. The minimum expected cell frequency is 48,6.

What do you value most from a flight?

	Observed N	Expected N	Residual
On-board service	100	60,0	40,0
Online Check-In	90	60,0	30,0
Online booking	50	60,0	-10,0
Cabin comfort (legroom etc.)	68	60,0	8,0
Luggage weight tolerance	35	60,0	-25,0
Something else:	17	60,0	-43,0
Total	360		

Test Statistics

	What do you value most from a flight?
Chi-square	85,633[a]
df	5
Asymp. Sig.	,000

Test Statistics

	What do you value most from a flight?
Chi-square	85,633[a]
df	5
Asymp. Sig.	,000

a. 0 cells (,0%) have expected frequencies less than 5. The minimum expected cell frequency is 60,0.

References

Adams, J., Khan, H., Raeside, R. and White, D. (2007) *Research Methods for Graduate Business and Social Science Students,* London: Sage Publications.

Aksoy, S., Atilgan, E. and Akinci, S. (2003) "Airline Services Marketing by Domestic and Foreign Firms: Differences From the Customers' Viewpoint", *Air Transport Management,* Vol. 9, pp. 343-351.

Allen, M., Titsworth, S. and Hunt, S. (2008) *Quantitative Research in Communication,* London: Sage.

Allen, P. and Bennett, K. (2010) *PSAW Statistics by SPSS – A Practical Guide – Version 18,* Melbourne: Cengage Learning Australia.

Alves, C. and Barbot, C. (2010) "Rivalry amongst European low-cost airlines: Are shareholders enjoying the game?", *Journal of Air Transport Management,* Vol. 16, pp. 304-309.

Basu, R. (2009) *Implementing Six Sigma and Lean – A Practical Guide to Tools and Techniques,* Oxford: Butterworth-Heinemann.

BATA (2010) *UK Airlines' Activity 1997 – 2010,* available at: http://www.caa.co.uk/default.aspx?categoryid=80 [accessed: 05.06.2011].

Bell, J. (2005) *Doing Your Research Project,* 4th Edition, Buckingham: Open University Press.

Beth, J. (1994) "Prove Public Relations Affects the Bottom Line", *The Public Relations Journal,* Vol. 50 (4), p. 40-41.

Biemer, P. and Lyberg, L. (2003) *Introduction to Survey Quality,* New Jersey: John Wiley & Sons.

Black, K. (2010) *Business Statistics: Contemporary Decision Making,* 6th Edition, Jefferson City: John Wiley & Sons.

Blaxter, L., Hughes, C. and Tight, M. (2006) *How to Research,* 3rd Edition, Maidenhead: McGraw-Hill.

Bryman, A. and Bell, E. (2007) *Business Research Methods,* 2nd Edition, New York: Oxford University Press.

Callison, C. and Seltzer, T. (2010) "Influence of Responsiveness, Accessibility and Professionalism on Journalists Perceptions of Southwest Airlines Public Relations", *Public Relations Review,* Vol. 36, pp. 141-146.

Carver, R. and Nash, J. (2009) *Doing Data Analysis with SPSS, Version 18: Version 18.0,* Boston: Cengage Learning.

Chan, K., Li, L., Diehl, S. and Terlutter, R. (2007) "Consumers Response to Offensive Advertising: A Cross Cultural Study", *International Marketing Review,* Vol. 24 (5), pp. 606-628.

Chang, Y.-W. and Chang, Y.-H. (2010) "Does Service Recovery Affect Satisfaction and Customer Loyalty? An Empirical Study of Airline Services", *Journal of Air Transport Management,* Vol. 16, pp. 340-342.

Chiou, Y. and Chen, Y. (2010) "Factors Influencing the Intentions of Passengers Regarding Full Service and Low Cost Carriers: A Note", *Journal of Air Transport Management,* Vol. 16, pp. 226-228.

Christen, C. (2005) "The Restructuring and Reengineering of AT&T: Analysis of a Public Relations Crisis using Organizational Theory", *Public Relations Review,* Vol. 31, pp. 239-251.

Cooper, D. and Schindler, P. (2006) *Business Research Methods,* 9th Edition, New York: McGraw-Hill.

Creaton, S. (2004) *Ryanair – How a Small Irish Airline Conquered Europe,* London: Aurum Press.

Creswell, J. (2009) *Research Design: Qualitative, Quantitative and Mixed Methods Approaches,* 3rd Edition, London: Sage.

Davies, B. (2007) *Doing a Successful Research Project: Using Qualitative or Quantitative Methods,* New York: Palgrave MacMillan.

Davison, L. and Ryley, T. (2010) "Tourism Destination Preferences of Low-Cost Airline Users in the East Midlands", *Journal of Transport Geography,* Vol. 18, pp. 458-465.

Dobruszkes, F. (2006) "An Analysis of European Low-Cost Airlines and their Networks", *Journal of Transport Geography,* Vol. 14, pp. 249-264.

Doganis, R. (2006) *The Airline Business,* 2nd Edition, New York: Routledge.

Dolnicar, S., Krabler, K., Grün, B. and Kulnig, A. (2011) "Key Drivers of Airline Loyalty", *Tourism Management,* Vol. 32, pp. 1020-1026.

Downing, J. (2004) "American Airlines' Use of Mediated Employee Channels After the 9/11 Attacks", *Public Relations Review,* Vol. 30, pp. 37-48.

Edwards, P., Roberts, I., Clarke, M., Di Guiseppe, C., Pratap, S., Wentz, R. and Kwan, I. (2002) "Increasing Response Rates to Postal Questionnaires: Systematic Review", *British Medical Journal,* Vol. 324, pp. 1183-91.

Engel, R. and Schutt, R. (2005) *The Practice of Research in Social Work,* London: Sage Publications.

Euromonitor International (2009) *Easygroup Ltd – Travel and Tourism – World,* available at: http://www.portal.euromonitor.com/Portal/Handlers/accessPDF.ashx?c=99\PDF\&f=F-122500-15871399.pdf&code=aav8%2biFx708lAgxvEV0ffiFuMfU%3d [accessed: 07.06.2011].

Euromonitor International (2010a) *Travel and Tourism – United Kingdom,* available at: http://ezproxy.napier.ac.uk:2102/Portal/Handlers/accessPDF.ashx?c=12\PDF\&f=F-156688-18238612.pdf&code=4fCAZ5tCqqzcbffZpotybETStBc%3d [accessed: 07.06.2011].

Euromonitor International (2010b) *Consumer Lifestyles – United Kingdom,* available at: http://www.portal.euromonitor.com/Portal/Handlers/accessPDF.ashx?c=45\PDF\&f=F-167970-19032845.pdf&code=T6anAp7EvqsmVyxac4PM5Q2TY34%3d [accessed: 14.06.2011].

Euromonitor International (2011) *Ryanair Holdings Plc in Travel and Tourism (World),* available at: http://www.portal.euromonitor.com/Portal/Handlers/accessPDF.ashx?c=88\PDF\&f=F-180277-19989688.pdf&code=RQW9rbLSHiyGlTcOUuOWlcVGUl8%3d [accessed: 07.06.2011].

Evans, M., Jamal, A. and Foxhall, G. (2006) *Consumer Behaviour,* Chichester: John Wiley & Sons Ltd.

Forgas, S., Moliner, M., Sánchez, J. and Palau, R. (2010) "Antecedents of Airline Passenger Loyalty: Low-cost versus Traditional Airlines", *Journal of Air Transport Management,* Vol. 16, pp. 229-233.

Financial Times (2011a) *Ryanair Results Disappoint O'Leary,* available at: https://ezp.napier.ac.uk/login?url=http://search.proquest.com/docview/848638982?accountid=16607 [accessed: 08.06.2011].

Financial Times (2011b) *"Disappointing" Loss at Ryanair,* available at: https://ezp.napier.ac.uk/login?url=http://search.proquest.com/docview/848638993?accountid=16607 [accessed: 08.06.2011].

Fine, L. (2009) *The SWOT Analysis: Using Your Strength to Overcome Weaknesses,* Seattle: CreateSpace.

Forbes, P. (1992) "Applying Strategic Management to Public Relations", *The Public Relations Journal,* Vol. 48 (3), p. 32.

Gallarza, M. and Saura, G. (2006) "Value Dimensions, Perceived Value, Satisfaction and Loyalty: An Investigation of University Students' Travel Behaviour", *Tourism Management,* Vol. 27, pp. 437-452.

Gountas, J. and Gountas, S. (2007) "Personality Orientations, Emotional States, Customer Satisfaction and Intention to Repurchase", *Journal of Business Research,* Vol. 60, pp. 72-75.

Greer, C. and Moreland, K. (2003) "United Airlines' and American Airlines' online crisis communication following the September 11 terrorist attacks", *Public Relations Review,* Vol. 29, pp. 427-441.

Hauss, D. (1993) "Measuring the Impact of Public Relations", *The Public Relations Journal,* Vol. 49 (2), p. 14.

Haywood, R. (1991) *All About Public Relations,* 2nd Edition, Berkshire: McGraw-Hill.

Hess, S. and Adler, T. (2011) "An Analysis of Trends in Air Travel Behaviour Using Four Related SP Datasets Collected Between 2000 and 2005", *Journal of Air Transport Management,* Vol. 17, pp. 244-248.

Hoy, W. (2009) *Quantitative Research in Education: A Primer,* London: Sage.

Hussey, J. and Hussey, R. (1997) *Business Research: A Practical Guide for Undergraduate and Postgraduate Students,* London: MacMillan Press.

Iarossy, G. (2006) *The Power of Survey Design,* Washington: The World Bank.

Jen, W., Tu, R. and Lu, T. (2011) "Managing Passenger Behavioural Intention: An Integrated Framework for Service Quality, Satisfaction, Perceived Value and Switching Barriers", *Transportation,* Vol. 38, pp. 321-342.

Jobber, D. (2010) *Principles and Practices of Marketing,* 6th Edition, London: McGraw-Hill.

Jones, L. (2007) *easyJet – The Story of Britain's Biggest Low-Cost Airline,* 2nd Edition, London: Aurum Press.

Koo, B., Mantin, B. and O'Connor, P. (2011) "Online Distribution of Airline Tickets: Should Airlines Adopt a Single or a Multi-Channel approach?", *Tourism Management,* Vol. 32, pp. 69-74.

L'Etang, J., Falkheimer, J. and Lugo, J. (2007) "Public Relations and Tourism: Critical Reflections and a Research Agenda", *Public Relations Review,* Vol. 33, pp. 68-76.

Mason, K. and Alamdari, F. (2007) "EU Network Carriers, Low Cost Carriers and Consumer Behaviour: A Delphi Study of Future Trends", *Journal of Air Transport Management,* Vol. 13, pp. 299-310.

Mudie, P. and Pirrie, A. (2006) *Services Marketing Management,* 3rd Edition, Oxford: Butterworth-Heinemann.

Macleod, S. (2010) "The Evolution of PR on the Internet", *Journal of Communication Management,* Vol. 5 (2), pp. 179-188.

Ni, N. (2006) "Relationships as organizational resources: Examining Public Relations impact through its connection with organizational strategies", *Public Relations Review,* Vol. 32, pp. 276-281.

Oliver, R. (1997) "Whence consumer loyalty?", *Journal of Marketing*, Vol. 63, pp. 33-45.

Pelsmacker, P. Geuens, M. and Bergh, J. (2010) *Marketing Communications – A European Perspective,* 4th edition, Pearson: Essex.

Reals, K. (2011) "Ryanair Comes to Town", *Airline Business,* Vol. 27 (1), pp. 28-31.

Ruddock, A. (2007) *Michael O'Leary – A Life in Full Flight,* London: Penguin Group.

Ruiz-Mafé, C., Sanz-Blas, S. and Aldás-Manzano, J. (2009) "Drivers and barriers to online airline ticket purchasing", *Journal of Air Transport Management,* Vol. 15, pp. 294-298.

Saunders, M., Lewis, P. and Thornhill, A. (2009) *Research Methods for Business Students,* 5th Edition, Essex: Pearson Education.

Shaw, S. (2007) *Airline Marketing and Management,* 6th Edition, London: Ashgate Publishing.

Shi, N. and Tao, J. (2008) *Statistical Hypothesis Testing,* Singapore: World Scientific Publishing.

Singleton, D. (2010) "Segmentation Reexamined", *Marketing Management,* Vol. 19 (4), pp. 20.

Sterne, J. (2000) *Customer Service on the Internet,* 2nd Edition, New York: John Wiley & Sons.

Swanborn, P. (2010) *Case Study Research: What, Why and How?,* London: Sage Publications.

Tench, R. and Yeomans, L. (2009) *Exploring Public Relations,* 2nd Edition, Harlow: Prentice Hall.

Tuzovic, S. (2010) "Frequent (flier) Frustration and the Dark Side of World-of-Web: Exploring Online Dysfunctional Behaviour in Online Feedback Forums", *Journal of Services Marketing,* Vol. 24 (6), pp. 446-457.

Vogel, A. (1994) "Model Aids in Cost-Effective Communications", *The Public Relations Journal,* Vol. 50 (2), p. 8.

Vogt, W. (2007) *Quantitative Research Methods for Professionals,* London: Pearson Education.

Wright, R. (2006) *Consumer Behaviour,* London: Thomson Learning.

Xavier, R., Johnston, K., Patel, A., Watson, T. and Simmons, P. (2005) "Using evaluation techniques and performance claims to demonstrate public relations impact: An Australian perspective", *Public Relations Review,* Vol. 31, pp. 417-424.

Yin, R. (2009) *Case Study Research: Design and Methods,* London: Sage Publications.